MUSHI

OF

OHIO

IDENTIFICATION
RECORD BOOK

Hello Wild

Your Feedback is Appreciated!!!

Please consider leaving us "5 Stars" on your Amazon review.

Thank you!

MUSHROOMS OF OHIO

This Mushrooom Identification Record Book
Belongs To:

_____

There are thousands of species of mushrooms in the Buckeye State. With a climate that is a variety of seasonal humid subtropical with cool winters and long, hot summers, a wide variety of mushrooms grow and thrive in the landscape. While many types are highly toxic, there are a number of edible mushrooms as well. Do not eat any mushroom without checking in person with a local, live mushroom collector/expert.

Use this record book to identify and record the many types of mushrooms you come across!

Location

Site / GPS: _____ Date: _____

○ Living Tree　○ Leaf Litter　○ Mulch　○ Dead Tree or Wood　○ Grass
○ Soil　○ Other _____

Type of Tree(s) On or Near: _____

Forest Type:　○ Deciduous　○ Coniferous　○ Tropical　○ Other _____

Weather Conditions: _____

General

Size (overall height): _____　Color: _____　Spore Color: _____

Texture:　○ Tough　○ Brittle　○ Leathery　○ Woody　○ Soft　○ Slimy
○ Spongy　○ Powdery　○ Waxy　○ Rubbery　○ Watery　(Other) _____

Bruising When Touched?　○ Yes　○ No　　Notes: _____

Structures:　○ Cup　○ Ring　○ Warts _____

Cap Characteristics

Campanulate
(bell-shaped)

Conical
(triangular)

Cylindrical
(shaped like half an egg)

Convex
(outwardly rounded)

Flat
(with top of
uniform height)

Infundibuliform
(deeply, depressed,
funnel-shaped)

Depressed
(with a low
central region)

Umbonate
(with a central
bump or knob)

Surface Markings (warts, scales, slime, etc.): _____

Cap Margin: Smooth, Inrolled, Sinuous/Wavy, Other: _____

Color Changes: _____

Undercap

Gills ○
Attachment: Free or Decurrent
Spacing: Crowded, Close,
　　　　　Distant, Subdistant
Color/Bruising: _____

Pores ○
Color: _____
Pore Size: _____
Pore Pattern: _____

Teeth ○
Color: _____
Teeth Length: _____
Flesh: Soft or Tough

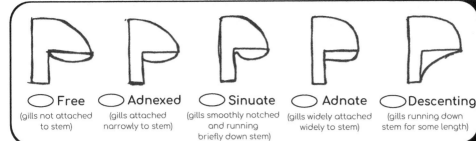

○ Free
(gills not attached to stem)

○ Adnexed
(gills attached narrowly to stem)

○ Sinuate
(gills smoothly notched and running briefly down stem)

○ Adnate
(gills widely attached widely to stem)

○ Descenting
(gills running down stem for some length)

  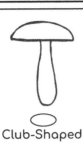   

○ Tapering

○ Equal

○ Club-Shaped

○ Bulbous

○ Cup (volva)

Chanterelle
- Edible ☺
- Shape looks like bell of a trumpet
- Bright yellow/orange
- Similar look to Jack o'Lantern

Shaggy Mane
- Edible ☺
- White shaggy cylindrical cap that turns black and inky with age
- Bell shape when mature
- Spore print is black

Morels
- Edible ☺
- Honeycombed cap
- Most morels cap is longer than stem
- Spore print is usually light colored
- Interior is hollow

Puffballs
- Edible ☺
- Color is white
- Rounded-shaped balls with or without spiny warts on top
- Can be mistaken for golf ball, baseball or even soccer ball

Meadow Mushroom
- Edible ☺
- White or whitish
- Pink gills that turn brown with age
- Closely related to portobello

False Morel
- Poisonous ☹
- Red-brown cap is irregularly lobed, like a brain
- Hollow chambers inside the cap
- Yellowish spore print

Fly Agaric
- Poisonous ☹
- Body emerges from soil looking like white eggs and turns red as it grows
- Small white to yellow pyramid-shaped warts

False Parasol
- Poisonous ☹
- White gills with no spores or green gills with green spores
- White to light brown stem

Jack O'Lantern
- Poisonous ☹
- Bright orange to yellowish
- Grows in clusters
- Cap convex
- Gills narrow
- Cream spore print

Destroying Angel
- Poisonous ☹
- White stalk and gills
- White cap or white edge and yellowish, pinkish, or tan center
- Egg-shaped cap

Shaggy Parasol
- Edible ☺
- Thick, fleshy scales on top of cap
- White spores
- White cap
- White gills
- Uniformly colored

Slippery Jack
- Edible ☺
- Brown cap, shiny and slimy when wet
- Dark chestnut brown
- Smooth semi-matt finish in summer

Spore Print

Location

Site / GPS: _____ Date: _____

○ Living Tree   ○ Leaf Litter   ○ Mulch   ○ Dead Tree or Wood   ○ Grass
○ Soil   ○ Other _____

Type of Tree(s) On or Near: _____

Forest Type: ○ Deciduous   ○ Coniferous   ○ Tropical   ○ Other _____

Weather Conditions: _____

General

Size (overall height): _____   Color: _____   Spore Color: _____

Texture: ○ Tough ○ Brittle ○ Leathery ○ Woody ○ Soft ○ Slimy
○ Spongy   ○ Powdery   ○ Waxy   ○ Rubbery   ○ Watery   (Other) _____

Bruising When Touched? ○ Yes ○ No   Notes: _____

Structures: ○ Cup ○ Ring ○ Warts   _____

Cap Characteristics

Campanulate
(bell-shaped)

Conical
(triangular)

Cylindrical
(shaped like half an egg)

Convex
(outwardly rounded)

Flat
(with top of
uniform height)

Infundibuliform
(deeply, depressed,
funnel-shaped)

Depressed
(with a low
central region)

Umbonate
(with a central
bump or knob)

Surface Markings (warts, scales, slime, etc.): _____

Cap Margin: Smooth, Inrolled, Sinuous/Wavy, Other: _____

Color Changes: _____

Undercap

Gills ○

Attachment: Free or Decurrent

Spacing: Crowded, Close,
Distant, Subdistant

Color/Bruising: _____

Pores ○

Color: _____

Pore Size: _____

Pore Pattern: _____

Teeth ○

Color: _____

Teeth Length: _____

Flesh: Soft or Tough

○ Free
(gills not attached to stem)

 ○ Adnexed
(gills attached narrowly to stem)

 ○ Sinuate
(gills smoothly notched and running briefly down stem)

 ○ Adnate
(gills widely attached widely to stem)

 ○ Descending
(gills running down stem for some length)

 Tapering

 Equal

 Club-Shaped

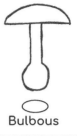 Bulbous

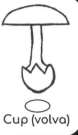 Cup (volva)

Chanterelle
- Edible ☺
- Shape looks like bell of a trumpet
- Bright yellow/orange
- Similar look to Jack o'Lantern

Shaggy Mane
- Edible ☺
- White shaggy cylindrical cap that turns black and inky with age
- Bell shape when mature
- Spore print is black

Morels
- Edible ☺
- Honeycombed cap
- Most morels cap is longer than stem
- Spore print is usually light colored
- Interior is hollow

Puffballs
- Edible ☺
- Color is white
- Rounded-shaped balls with or without spiny warts on top
- Can be mistaken for golf ball, baseball or even soccer ball

Meadow Mushroom
- Edible ☺
- White or whitish
- Pink gills that turn brown with age
- Closely related to portobello

False Morel
- Poisonous ☹
- Red-brown cap is irregularly lobed, like a brain
- Hollow chambers inside the cap
- Yellowish spore print

Fly Agaric
- Poisonous ☹
- Body emerges from soil looking like white eggs and turns red as it grows
- Small white to yellow pyramid-shaped warts

False Parasol
- Poisonous ☹
- White gills with no spores or green gills with green spores
- White to light brown stem

Jack O'Lantern
- Poisonous ☹
- Bright orange to yellowish
- Grows in clusters
- Cap convex
- Gills narrow
- Cream spore print

Destroying Angel
- Poisonous ☹
- White stalk and gills
- White cap or white edge and yellowish, pinkish, or tan center
- Egg-shaped cap

Shaggy Parasol
- Edible ☺
- Thick, fleshy scales on top of cap
- White spores
- White cap
- White gills
- Uniformly colored

Slippery Jack
- Edible ☺
- Brown cap, shiny and slimy when wet
- Dark chestnut brown
- Smooth semi-matt finish in summer

Spore Print

_____
_____
_____
_____
_____
_____

Location

Site / GPS: _____ Date: _____

○ Living Tree ○ Leaf Litter ○ Mulch ○ Dead Tree or Wood ○ Grass
○ Soil ○ Other _____

Type of Tree(s) On or Near: _____

Forest Type: ○ Deciduous ○ Coniferous ○ Tropical ○ Other _____

Weather Conditions: _____

General

Size (overall height): _____ Color: _____ Spore Color: _____

Texture: ○ Tough ○ Brittle ○ Leathery ○ Woody ○ Soft ○ Slimy
○ Spongy ○ Powdery ○ Waxy ○ Rubbery ○ Watery (Other) _____

Bruising When Touched? ○ Yes ○ No   Notes: _____

Structures: ○ Cup ○ Ring ○ Warts   _____

Cap Characteristics

Campanulate
(bell-shaped)

Conical
(triangular)

Cylindrical
(shaped like half an egg)

Convex
(outwardly rounded)

Flat
(with top of
uniform height)

Infundibuliform
(deeply, depressed,
funnel-shaped)

Depressed
(with a low
central region)

Umbonate
(with a central
bump or knob)

Surface Markings (warts, scales, slime, etc.): _____

Cap Margin: Smooth, Inrolled, Sinuous/Wavy, Other: _____

Color Changes: _____

Undercap

Gills ○
Attachment: Free or Decurrent
Spacing: Crowded, Close,
Distant, Subdistant
Color/Bruising: _____

Pores ○
Color: _____
Pore Size: _____
Pore Pattern: _____

Teeth ○
Color: _____
Teeth Length: _____
Flesh: Soft or Tough

○ Free
(gills not attached to stem)

○ Adnexed
(gills attached narrowly to stem)

○ Sinuate
(gills smoothly notched and running briefly down stem)

○ Adnate
(gills widely attached widely to stem)

○ Descenting
(gills running down stem for some length)

  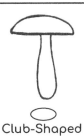 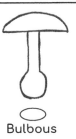 

Tapering   Equal   Club-Shaped   Bulbous   Cup (volva)

Chanterelle
- Edible ☺
- Shape looks like bell of a trumpet
- Bright yellow/orange
- Similar look to Jack o'Lantern

Shaggy Mane
- Edible ☺
- White shaggy cylindrical cap that turns black and inky with age
- Bell shape when mature
- Spore print is black

Morels
- Edible ☺
- Honeycombed cap
- Most morels cap is longer than stem
- Spore print is usually light colored
- Interior is hollow

Puffballs
- Edible ☺
- Color is white
- Rounded-shaped balls with or without spiny warts on top
- Can be mistaken for golf ball, baseball or even soccer ball

Meadow Mushroom
- Edible ☺
- White or whitish
- Pink gills that turn brown with age
- Closely related to portobello

False Morel
- Poisonous ☹
- Red-brown cap is irregularly lobed, like a brain
- Hollow chambers inside the cap
- Yellowish spore print

Fly Agaric
- Poisonous ☹
- Body emerges from soil looking like white eggs and turns red as it grows
- Small white to yellow pyramid-shaped warts

False Parasol
- Poisonous ☹
- White gills with no spores or green gills with green spores
- White to light brown stem

Jack O'Lantern
- Poisonous ☹
- Bright orange to yellowish
- Grows in clusters
- Cap convex
- Gills narrow
- Cream spore print

Destroying Angel
- Poisonous ☹
- White stalk and gills
- White cap or white edge and yellowish, pinkish, or tan center
- Egg-shaped cap

Shaggy Parasol
- Edible ☺
- Thick, fleshy scales on top of cap
- White spores
- White cap
- White gills
- Uniformly colored

Slippery Jack
- Edible ☺
- Brown cap, shiny and slimy when wet
- Dark chestnut brown
- Smooth semi-matt finish in summer

Spore Print

Location

Site / GPS: _____ Date: _____

⊙ Living Tree ⊙ Leaf Litter ⊙ Mulch ⊙ Dead Tree or Wood ⊙ Grass
⊙ Soil ⊙ Other _____

Type of Tree(s) On or Near: _____

Forest Type: ⊙ Deciduous ⊙ Coniferous ⊙ Tropical ⊙ Other _____

Weather Conditions: _____

General

Size (overall height): _____ Color: _____ Spore Color: _____

Texture: ⊙ Tough ⊙ Brittle ⊙ Leathery ⊙ Woody ⊙ Soft ⊙ Slimy
⊙ Spongy ⊙ Powdery ⊙ Waxy ⊙ Rubbery ⊙ Watery (Other) _____

Bruising When Touched? ⊙ Yes ⊙ No   Notes: _____

Structures: ⊙ Cup ⊙ Ring ⊙ Warts   _____

Cap Characteristics

Campanulate
(bell-shaped)

Conical
(triangular)

Cylindrical
(shaped like half an egg)

Convex
(outwardly rounded)

Flat
(with top of uniform height)

Infundibuliform
(deeply, depressed, funnel-shaped)

Depressed
(with a low central region)

Umbonate
(with a central bump or knob)

Surface Markings (warts, scales, slime, etc.): _____

Cap Margin: Smooth, Inrolled, Sinuous/Wavy, Other:_____

Color Changes: _____

Undercap

Gills ⊙
Attachment: Free or Decurrent
Spacing: Crowded, Close, Distant, Subdistant
Color/Bruising: _____

Pores ⊙
Color: _____
Pore Size: _____
Pore Pattern: _____

Teeth ⊙
Color: _____
Teeth Length: _____
Flesh: Soft or Tough

Free	Adnexed	Sinuate	Adnate	Descenting
(gills not attached to stem)	(gills attached narrowly to stem)	(gills smoothly notched and running briefly down stem)	(gills widely attached widely to stem)	(gills running down stem for some length)

   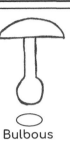 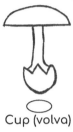

| Tapering | Equal | Club-Shaped | Bulbous | Cup (volva) |

Chanterelle
- Edible ☺
- Shape looks like bell of a trumpet
- Bright yellow/orange
- Similar look to Jack o'Lantern

Shaggy Mane
- Edible ☺
- White shaggy cylindrical cap that turns black and inky with age
- Bell shape when mature
- Spore print is black

Morels
- Edible ☺
- Honeycombed cap
- Most morels cap is longer than stem
- Spore print is usually light colored
- Interior is hollow

Puffballs
- Edible ☺
- Color is white
- Rounded-shaped balls with or without spiny warts on top
- Can be mistaken for golf ball, baseball or even soccer ball

Meadow Mushroom
- Edible ☺
- White or whitish
- Pink gills that turn brown with age
- Closely related to portobello

False Morel
- Poisonous ☹
- Red-brown cap is irregularly lobed, like a brain
- Hollow chambers inside the cap
- Yellowish spore print

Fly Agaric
- Poisonous ☹
- Body emerges from soil looking like white eggs and turns red as it grows
- Small white to yellow pyramid-shaped warts

False Parasol
- Poisonous ☹
- White gills with no spores or green gills with green spores
- White to light brown stem

Jack O'Lantern
- Poisonous ☹
- Bright orange to yellowish
- Grows in clusters
- Cap convex
- Gills narrow
- Cream spore print

Destroying Angel
- Poisonous ☹
- White stalk and gills
- White cap or white edge and yellowish, pinkish, or tan center
- Egg-shaped cap

Shaggy Parasol
- Edible ☺
- Thick, fleshy scales on top of cap
- White spores
- White cap
- White gills
- Uniformly colored

Slippery Jack
- Edible ☺
- Brown cap, shiny and slimy when wet
- Dark chestnut brown
- Smooth semi-matt finish in summer

Spore Print

_____
_____
_____
_____
_____
_____

Location

Site / GPS: _____ Date: _____

◯ Living Tree ◯ Leaf Litter ◯ Mulch ◯ Dead Tree or Wood ◯ Grass
◯ Soil ◯ Other _____

Type of Tree(s) On or Near: _____

Forest Type: ◯ Deciduous ◯ Coniferous ◯ Tropical ◯ Other _____

Weather Conditions: _____

General

Size (overall height): _____ Color: _____ Spore Color: _____

Texture: ◯ Tough ◯ Brittle ◯ Leathery ◯ Woody ◯ Soft ◯ Slimy
◯ Spongy ◯ Powdery ◯ Waxy ◯ Rubbery ◯ Watery (Other) _____

Bruising When Touched? ◯ Yes ◯ No   Notes: _____

Structures: ◯ Cup ◯ Ring ◯ Warts   _____

Cap Characteristics

Campanulate
(bell-shaped)

Conical
(triangular)

Cylindrical
(shaped like half an egg)

Convex
(outwardly rounded)

Flat
(with top of
uniform height)

Infundibuliform
(deeply, depressed,
funnel-shaped)

Depressed
(with a low
central region)

Umbonate
(with a central
bump or knob)

Surface Markings (warts, scales, slime, etc.): _____

Cap Margin: Smooth, Inrolled, Sinuous/Wavy, Other: _____

Color Changes: _____

Undercap

Gills ◯

Attachment: Free or Decurrent

Spacing: Crowded, Close,
Distant, Subdistant

Color/Bruising: _____

Pores ◯

Color: _____

Pore Size: _____

Pore Pattern: _____

Teeth ◯

Color: _____

Teeth Length: _____

Flesh: Soft or Tough

○ **Free**
(gills not attached to stem)

○ **Adnexed**
(gills attached narrowly to stem)

○ **Sinuate**
(gills smoothly notched and running briefly down stem)

○ **Adnate**
(gills widely attached widely to stem)

○ **Descenting**
(gills running down stem for some length)

 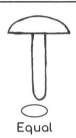  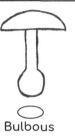 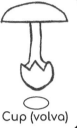

○ **Tapering**　　○ **Equal**　　○ **Club-Shaped**　　○ **Bulbous**　　○ **Cup (volva)**

Chanterelle
- Edible ☺
- Shape looks like bell of a trumpet
- Bright yellow/orange
- Similar look to Jack o'Lantern

Meadow Mushroom
- Edible ☺
- White or whitish
- Pink gills that turn brown with age
- Closely related to portobello

Jack O'Lantern
- Poisonous ☹
- Bright orange to yellowish
- Grows in clusters
- Cap convex
- Gills narrow
- Cream spore print

Shaggy Mane
- Edible ☺
- White shaggy cylindrical cap that turns black and inky with age
- Bell shape when mature
- Spore print is black

False Morel
- Poisonous ☹
- Red-brown cap is irregularly lobed, like a brain
- Hollow chambers inside the cap
- Yellowish spore print

Destroying Angel
- Poisonous ☹
- White stalk and gills
- White cap or white edge and yellowish, pinkish, or tan center
- Egg-shaped cap

Morels
- Edible ☺
- Honeycombed cap
- Most morels cap is longer than stem
- Spore print is usually light colored
- Interior is hollow

Fly Agaric
- Poisonous ☹
- Body emerges from soil looking like white eggs and turns red as it grows
- Small white to yellow pyramid-shaped warts

Shaggy Parasol
- Edible ☺
- Thick, fleshy scales on top of cap
- White spores
- White cap
- White gills
- Uniformly colored

Puffballs
- Edible ☺
- Color is white
- Rounded-shaped balls with or without spiny warts on top
- Can be mistaken for golf ball, baseball or even soccer ball

False Parasol
- Poisonous ☹
- White gills with no spores or green gills with green spores
- White to light brown stem

Slippery Jack
- Edible ☺
- Brown cap, shiny and slimy when wet
- Dark chestnut brown
- Smooth semi-matt finish in summer

Spore Print

_____
_____
_____
_____
_____
_____
_____

Location

Site / GPS: _____ Date: _____

○ Living Tree   ○ Leaf Litter   ○ Mulch   ○ Dead Tree or Wood   ○ Grass
○ Soil   ○ Other _____

Type of Tree(s) On or Near: _____

Forest Type: ○ Deciduous   ○ Coniferous   ○ Tropical   ○ Other _____

Weather Conditions: _____

General

Size (overall height): _____   Color: _____   Spore Color: _____

Texture: ○ Tough ○ Brittle ○ Leathery ○ Woody ○ Soft ○ Slimy
○ Spongy   ○ Powdery   ○ Waxy   ○ Rubbery   ○ Watery   (Other) _____

Bruising When Touched? ○ Yes ○ No   Notes: _____

Structures: ○ Cup ○ Ring ○ Warts   _____

Cap Characteristics

Campanulate
(bell-shaped)

Conical
(triangular)

Cylindrical
(shaped like half an egg)

Convex
(outwardly rounded)

Flat
(with top of
uniform height)

Infundibuliform
(deeply, depressed,
funnel-shaped)

Depressed
(with a low
central region)

Umbonate
(with a central
bump or knob)

Surface Markings (warts, scales, slime, etc.): _____

Cap Margin: Smooth, Inrolled, Sinuous/Wavy, Other:_____

Color Changes: _____

Undercap

Gills ○

Attachment: Free or Decurrent

Spacing: Crowded, Close,
         Distant, Subsistant

Color/Bruising: _____

Pores ○

Color: _____

Pore Size: _____

Pore Pattern: _____

Teeth ○

Color: _____

Teeth Length: _____

Flesh: Soft or Tough

○ **Free**
(gills not attached to stem)

○ **Adnexed**
(gills attached narrowly to stem)

○ **Sinuate**
(gills smoothly notched and running briefly down stem)

○ **Adnate**
(gills widely attached widely to stem)

○ **Descenting**
(gills running down stem for some length)

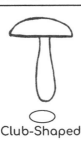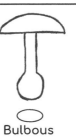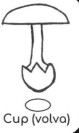

○ **Tapering**

○ **Equal**

○ **Club-Shaped**

○ **Bulbous**

○ **Cup (volva)**

Chanterelle
- Edible ☺
- Shape looks like bell of a trumpet
- Bright yellow/orange
- Similar look to Jack o'Lantern

Meadow Mushroom
- Edible ☺
- White or whitish
- Pink gills that turn brown with age
- Closely related to portobello

Jack O'Lantern
- Poisonous ☹
- Bright orange to yellowish
- Grows in clusters
- Cap convex
- Gills narrow
- Cream spore print

Shaggy Mane
- Edible ☺
- White shaggy cylindrical cap that turns black and inky with age
- Bell shape when mature
- Spore print is black

False Morel
- Poisonous ☹
- Red-brown cap is irregularly lobed, like a brain
- Hollow chambers inside the cap
- Yellowish spore print

Destroying Angel
- Poisonous ☹
- White stalk and gills
- White cap or white edge and yellowish, pinkish, or tan center
- Egg-shaped cap

Morels
- Edible ☺
- Honeycombed cap
- Most morels cap is longer than stem
- Spore print is usually light colored
- Interior is hollow

Fly Agaric
- Poisonous ☹
- Body emerges from soil looking like white eggs and turns red as it grows
- Small white to yellow pyramid-shaped warts

Shaggy Parasol
- Edible ☺
- Thick, fleshy scales on top of cap
- White spores
- White cap
- White gills
- Uniformly colored

Puffballs
- Edible ☺
- Color is white
- Rounded-shaped balls with or without spiny warts on top
- Can be mistaken for golf ball, baseball or even soccer ball

False Parasol
- Poisonous ☹
- White gills with no spores or green gills with green spores
- White to light brown stem

Slippery Jack
- Edible ☺
- Brown cap, shiny and slimy when wet
- Dark chestnut brown
- Smooth semi-matt finish in summer

Spore Print

_____
_____
_____
_____
_____
_____

Location

Site / GPS: _____ Date: _____

○ Living Tree ○ Leaf Litter ○ Mulch ○ Dead Tree or Wood ○ Grass
○ Soil ○ Other _____

Type of Tree(s) On or Near: _____

Forest Type: ○ Deciduous ○ Coniferous ○ Tropical ○ Other _____

Weather Conditions: _____

General

Size (overall height): _____ Color: _____ Spore Color: _____

Texture: ○ Tough ○ Brittle ○ Leathery ○ Woody ○ Soft ○ Slimy
○ Spongy ○ Powdery ○ Waxy ○ Rubbery ○ Watery (Other) _____

Bruising When Touched? ○ Yes ○ No   Notes: _____

Structures: ○ Cup ○ Ring ○ Warts   _____

Cap Characteristics

Campanulate
(bell-shaped)

Conical
(triangular)

Cylindrical
(shaped like half an egg)

Convex
(outwardly rounded)

Flat
(with top of
uniform height)

Infundibuliform
(deeply, depressed,
funnel-shaped)

Depressed
(with a low
central region)

Umbonate
(with a central
bump or knob)

Surface Markings (warts, scales, slime, etc.): _____

Cap Margin: Smooth, Inrolled, Sinuous/Wavy, Other: _____

Color Changes: _____

Undercap

Gills ○
Attachment: Free or Decurrent
Spacing: Crowded, Close,
    Distant, Subdistant
Color/Bruising: _____

Pores ○
Color: _____
Pore Size: _____
Pore Pattern: _____

Teeth ○
Color: _____
Teeth Length: _____
Flesh: Soft or Tough

○ Free
(gills not attached to stem)

○ Adnexed
(gills attached narrowly to stem)

○ Sinuate
(gills smoothly notched and running briefly down stem)

○ Adnate
(gills widely attached widely to stem)

○ Descenting
(gills running down stem for some length)

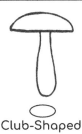
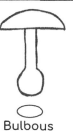
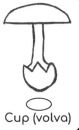

Tapering   Equal   Club-Shaped   Bulbous   Cup (volva)

Chanterelle
- Edible ☺
- Shape looks like bell of a trumpet
- Bright yellow/orange
- Similar look to Jack o'Lantern

Shaggy Mane
- Edible ☺
- White shaggy cylindrical cap that turns black and inky with age
- Bell shape when mature
- Spore print is black

Morels
- Edible ☺
- Honeycombed cap
- Most morels cap is longer than stem
- Spore print is usually light colored
- Interior is hollow

Puffballs
- Edible ☺
- Color is white
- Rounded-shaped balls with or without spiny warts on top
- Can be mistaken for golf ball, baseball or even soccer ball

Meadow Mushroom
- Edible ☺
- White or whitish
- Pink gills that turn brown with age
- Closely related to portobello

False Morel
- Poisonous ☹
- Red-brown cap is irregularly lobed, like a brain
- Hollow chambers inside the cap
- Yellowish spore print

Fly Agaric
- Poisonous ☹
- Body emerges from soil looking like white eggs and turns red as it grows
- Small white to yellow pyramid-shaped warts

False Parasol
- Poisonous ☹
- White gills with no spores or green gills with green spores
- White to light brown stem

Jack O'Lantern
- Poisonous ☹
- Bright orange to yellowish
- Grows in clusters
- Cap convex
- Gills narrow
- Cream spore print

Destroying Angel
- Poisonous ☹
- White stalk and gills
- White cap or white edge and yellowish, pinkish, or tan center
- Egg-shaped cap

Shaggy Parasol
- Edible ☺
- Thick, fleshy scales on top of cap
- White spores
- White cap
- White gills
- Uniformly colored

Slippery Jack
- Edible ☺
- Brown cap, shiny and slimy when wet
- Dark chestnut brown
- Smooth semi-matt finish in summer

Spore Print

_____
_____
_____
_____
_____
_____

Location

Site / GPS: _____ Date: _____

◯ Living Tree ◯ Leaf Litter ◯ Mulch ◯ Dead Tree or Wood ◯ Grass
◯ Soil ◯ Other _____

Type of Tree(s) On or Near: _____

Forest Type: ◯ Deciduous ◯ Coniferous ◯ Tropical ◯ Other _____

Weather Conditions: _____

General

Size (overall height): _____ Color: _____ Spore Color: _____

Texture: ◯ Tough ◯ Brittle ◯ Leathery ◯ Woody ◯ Soft ◯ Slimy
◯ Spongy ◯ Powdery ◯ Waxy ◯ Rubbery ◯ Watery (Other) _____

Bruising When Touched? ◯ Yes ◯ No   Notes: _____

Structures: ◯ Cup ◯ Ring ◯ Warts   _____

Cap Characteristics

Campanulate
(bell-shaped)

Conical
(triangular)

Cylindrical
(shaped like half an egg)

Convex
(outwardly rounded)

Flat
(with top of
uniform height)

Infundibuliform
(deeply, depressed,
funnel-shaped)

Depressed
(with a low
central region)

Umbonate
(with a central
bump or knob)

Surface Markings (warts, scales, slime, etc.): _____

Cap Margin: Smooth, Inrolled, Sinuous/Wavy, Other: _____

Color Changes: _____

Undercap

Gills ◯

Attachment: Free or Decurrent

Spacing: Crowded, Close,
           Distant, Subdistant

Color/Bruising: _____

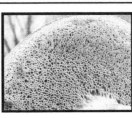

Pores ◯

Color: _____

Pore Size: _____

Pore Pattern: _____

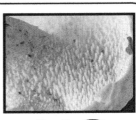

Teeth ◯

Color: _____

Teeth Length: _____

Flesh: Soft or Tough

◯ Free
(gills not attached to stem)

◯ Adnexed
(gills attached narrowly to stem)

◯ Sinuate
(gills smoothly notched and running briefly down stem)

◯ Adnate
(gills widely attached widely to stem)

◯ Descenting
(gills running down stem for some length)

  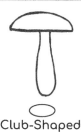 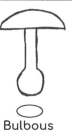 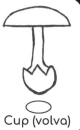

◯ Tapering

◯ Equal

◯ Club-Shaped

◯ Bulbous

◯ Cup (volva)

Chanterelle
- Edible 😊
- Shape looks like bell of a trumpet
- Bright yellow/orange
- Similar look to Jack o'Lantern

Shaggy Mane
- Edible 😊
- White shaggy cylindrical cap that turns black and inky with age
- Bell shape when mature
- Spore print is black

Morels
- Edible 😊
- Honeycombed cap
- Most morels cap is longer than stem
- Spore print is usually light colored
- Interior is hollow

Puffballs
- Edible 😊
- Color is white
- Rounded-shaped balls with or without spiny warts on top
- Can be mistaken for golf ball, baseball or even soccer ball

Meadow Mushroom
- Edible 😊
- White or whitish
- Pink gills that turn brown with age
- Closely related to portobello

False Morel
- Poisonous 😣
- Red-brown cap is irregularly lobed, like a brain
- Hollow chambers inside the cap
- Yellowish spore print

Fly Agaric
- Poisonous 😣
- Body emerges from soil looking like white eggs and turns red as it grows
- Small white to yellow pyramid-shaped warts

False Parasol
- Poisonous 😣
- White gills with no spores or green gills with green spores
- White to light brown stem

Jack O'Lantern
- Poisonous 😣
- Bright orange to yellowish
- Grows in clusters
- Cap convex
- Gills narrow
- Cream spore print

Destroying Angel
- Poisonous 😣
- White stalk and gills
- White cap or white edge and yellowish, pinkish, or tan center
- Egg-shaped cap

Shaggy Parasol
- Edible 😊
- Thick, fleshy scales on top of cap
- White spores
- White cap
- White gills
- Uniformly colored

Slippery Jack
- Edible 😊
- Brown cap, shiny and slimy when wet
- Dark chestnut brown
- Smooth semi-matt finish in summer

Spore Print

_____
_____
_____
_____
_____
_____

Location

Site / GPS: _____ Date: _____

◯ Living Tree ◯ Leaf Litter ◯ Mulch ◯ Dead Tree or Wood ◯ Grass

◯ Soil ◯ Other _____

Type of Tree(s) On or Near: _____

Forest Type: ◯ Deciduous ◯ Coniferous ◯ Tropical ◯ Other _____

Weather Conditions: _____

General

Size (overall height): _____ Color: _____ Spore Color: _____

Texture: ◯ Tough ◯ Brittle ◯ Leathery ◯ Woody ◯ Soft ◯ Slimy

◯ Spongy ◯ Powdery ◯ Waxy ◯ Rubbery ◯ Watery (Other) _____

Bruising When Touched? ◯ Yes ◯ No Notes: _____

Structures: ◯ Cup ◯ Ring ◯ Warts _____

Cap Characteristics

Campanulate
(bell-shaped)

Conical
(triangular)

Cylindrical
(shaped like half an egg)

Convex
(outwardly rounded)

Flat
(with top of
uniform height)

Infundibuliform
(deeply, depressed,
funnel-shaped)

Depressed
(with a low
central region)

Umbonate
(with a central
bump or knob)

Surface Markings (warts, scales, slime, etc.): _____

Cap Margin: Smooth, Inrolled, Sinuous/Wavy, Other: _____

Color Changes: _____

Undercap

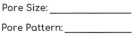

Gills ◯

Attachment: Free or Decurrent

Spacing: Crowded, Close,
Distant, Subdistant

Color/Bruising: _____

Pores ◯

Color: _____

Pore Size: _____

Pore Pattern: _____

Teeth ◯

Color: _____

Teeth Length: _____

Flesh: Soft or Tough

○ Free
(gills not attached to stem)

○ Adnexed
(gills attached narrowly to stem)

○ Sinuate
(gills smoothly notched and running briefly down stem)

○ Adnate
(gills widely attached widely to stem)

○ Descenting
(gills running down stem for some length)

   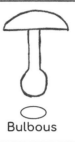 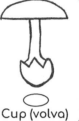

○ Tapering

○ Equal

○ Club-Shaped

○ Bulbous

○ Cup (volva)

Chanterelle

- Edible ☺
- Shape looks like bell of a trumpet
- Bright yellow/orange
- Similar look to Jack o'Lantern

Meadow Mushroom

- Edible ☺
- White or whitish
- Pink gills that turn brown with age
- Closely related to portobello

Jack O'Lantern

- Poisonous ☹
- Bright orange to yellowish
- Grows in clusters
- Cap convex
- Gills narrow
- Cream spore print

Shaggy Mane

- Edible ☺
- White shaggy cylindrical cap that turns black and inky with age
- Bell shape when mature
- Spore print is black

False Morel

- Poisonous ☹
- Red-brown cap is irregularly lobed, like a brain
- Hollow chambers inside the cap
- Yellowish spore print

Destroying Angel

- Poisonous ☹
- White stalk and gills
- White cap or white edge and yellowish, pinkish, or tan center
- Egg-shaped cap

Morels

- Edible ☺
- Honeycombed cap
- Most morels cap is longer than stem
- Spore print is usually light colored
- Interior is hollow

Fly Agaric

- Poisonous ☹
- Body emerges from soil looking like white eggs and turns red as it grows
- Small white to yellow pyramid-shaped warts

Shaggy Parasol

- Edible ☺
- Thick, fleshy scales on top of cap
- White spores
- White cap
- White gills
- Uniformly colored

Puffballs

- Edible ☺
- Color is white
- Rounded-shaped balls with or without spiny warts on top
- Can be mistaken for golf ball, baseball or even soccer ball

False Parasol

- Poisonous ☹
- White gills with no spores or green gills with green spores
- White to light brown stem

Slippery Jack

- Edible ☺
- Brown cap, shiny and slimy when wet
- Dark chestnut brown
- Smooth semi-matt finish in summer

Spore Print

_____

_____

_____

_____

_____

_____

Location

Site / GPS: _____ Date: _____

◯ Living Tree   ◯ Leaf Litter   ◯ Mulch   ◯ Dead Tree or Wood   ◯ Grass
◯ Soil   ◯ Other _____

Type of Tree(s) On or Near: _____

Forest Type: ◯ Deciduous   ◯ Coniferous   ◯ Tropical   ◯ Other _____

Weather Conditions: _____

General

Size (overall height): _____   Color: _____   Spore Color: _____

Texture: ◯ Tough ◯ Brittle ◯ Leathery ◯ Woody ◯ Soft ◯ Slimy
◯ Spongy ◯ Powdery ◯ Waxy ◯ Rubbery ◯ Watery (Other) _____

Bruising When Touched? ◯ Yes ◯ No   Notes: _____

Structures: ◯ Cup ◯ Ring ◯ Warts   _____

Cap Characteristics

Campanulate
(bell-shaped)

Conical
(triangular)

Cylindrical
(shaped like half an egg)

Convex
(outwardly rounded)

Flat
(with top of
uniform height)

Infundibuliform
(deeply, depressed,
funnel-shaped)

Depressed
(with a low
central region)

Umbonate
(with a central
bump or knob)

Surface Markings (warts, scales, slime, etc.): _____

Cap Margin: Smooth, Inrolled, Sinuous/Wavy, Other: _____

Color Changes: _____

Undercap

Gills ◯

Attachment: Free or Decurrent

Spacing: Crowded, Close,
Distant, Subdistant

Color/Bruising: _____

Pores ◯

Color: _____

Pore Size: _____

Pore Pattern: _____

Teeth ◯

Color: _____

Teeth Length: _____

Flesh: Soft or Tough

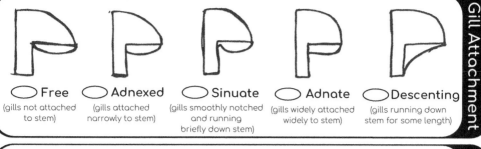

○ **Free**
(gills not attached to stem)

○ **Adnexed**
(gills attached narrowly to stem)

○ **Sinuate**
(gills smoothly notched and running briefly down stem)

○ **Adnate**
(gills widely attached widely to stem)

○ **Descenting**
(gills running down stem for some length)

○ **Tapering** ○ **Equal** ○ **Club-Shaped** ○ **Bulbous** ○ **Cup (volva)**

Chanterelle

- Edible ☺
- Shape looks like bell of a trumpet
- Bright yellow/orange
- Similar look to Jack o'Lantern

Meadow Mushroom

- Edible ☺
- White or whitish
- Pink gills that turn brown with age
- Closely related to portobello

Jack O'Lantern

- Poisonous ☹
- Bright orange to yellowish
- Grows in clusters
- Cap convex
- Gills narrow
- Cream spore print

Shaggy Mane

- Edible ☺
- White shaggy cylindrical cap that turns black and inky with age
- Bell shape when mature
- Spore print is black

False Morel

- Poisonous ☹
- Red-brown cap is irregularly lobed, like a brain
- Hollow chambers inside the cap
- Yellowish spore print

Destroying Angel

- Poisonous ☹
- White stalk and gills
- White cap or white edge and yellowish, pinkish, or tan center
- Egg-shaped cap

Morels

- Edible ☺
- Honeycombed cap
- Most morels cap is longer than stem
- Spore print is usually light colored
- Interior is hollow

Fly Agaric

- Poisonous ☹
- Body emerges from soil looking like white eggs and turns red as it grows
- Small white to yellow pyramid-shaped warts

Shaggy Parasol

- Edible ☺
- Thick, fleshy scales on top of cap
- White spores
- White cap
- White gills
- Uniformly colored

Puffballs

- Edible ☺
- Color is white
- Rounded-shaped balls with or without spiny warts on top
- Can be mistaken for golf ball, baseball or even soccer ball

False Parasol

- Poisonous ☹
- White gills with no spores or green gills with green spores
- White to light brown stem

Slippery Jack

- Edible ☺
- Brown cap, shiny and slimy when wet
- Dark chestnut brown
- Smooth semi-matt finish in summer

Spore Print

_____

_____
_____
_____
_____
_____
_____

Location

Site / GPS: _____ Date: _____

○ Living Tree ○ Leaf Litter ○ Mulch ○ Dead Tree or Wood ○ Grass
○ Soil ○ Other _____

Type of Tree(s) On or Near: _____

Forest Type: ○ Deciduous ○ Coniferous ○ Tropical ○ Other _____

Weather Conditions: _____

General

Size (overall height): _____ Color: _____ Spore Color: _____

Texture: ○ Tough ○ Brittle ○ Leathery ○ Woody ○ Soft ○ Slimy
○ Spongy ○ Powdery ○ Waxy ○ Rubbery ○ Watery (Other) _____

Bruising When Touched? ○ Yes ○ No Notes: _____

Structures: ○ Cup ○ Ring ○ Warts _____

Cap Characteristics

Campanulate
(bell-shaped)

Conical
(triangular)

Cylindrical
(shaped like half an egg)

Convex
(outwardly rounded)

Flat
(with top of
uniform height)

Infundibuliform
(deeply, depressed,
funnel-shaped)

Depressed
(with a low
central region)

Umbonate
(with a central
bump or knob)

Surface Markings (warts, scales, slime, etc.): _____

Cap Margin: Smooth, Inrolled, Sinuous/Wavy, Other:_____

Color Changes: _____

Undercap

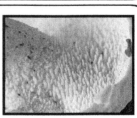

Gills ○

Attachment: Free or Decurrent

Spacing: Crowded, Close,
Distant, Subdistant

Color/Bruising: _____

Pores ○

Color: _____

Pore Size: _____

Pore Pattern: _____

Teeth ○

Color: _____

Teeth Length: _____

Flesh: Soft or Tough

○ Free
(gills not attached to stem)

○ Adnexed
(gills attached narrowly to stem)

○ Sinuate
(gills smoothly notched and running briefly down stem)

○ Adnate
(gills widely attached widely to stem)

○ Descending
(gills running down stem for some length)

   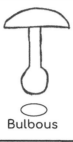  

○ Tapering

○ Equal

○ Club-Shaped

○ Bulbous

○ Cup (volva)

Chanterelle

- Edible ☺
- Shape looks like bell of a trumpet
- Bright yellow/orange
- Similar look to Jack o'Lantern

Shaggy Mane

- Edible ☺
- White shaggy cylindrical cap that turns black and inky with age
- Bell shape when mature
- Spore print is black

Morels

- Edible ☺
- Honeycombed cap
- Most morels cap is longer than stem
- Spore print is usually light colored
- Interior is hollow

Puffballs

- Edible ☺
- Color is white
- Rounded-shaped balls with or without spiny warts on top
- Can be mistaken for golf ball, baseball or even soccer ball

Meadow Mushroom

- Edible ☺
- White or whitish
- Pink gills that turn brown with age
- Closely related to portobello

False Morel

- Poisonous ☹
- Red-brown cap is irregularly lobed, like a brain
- Hollow chambers inside the cap
- Yellowish spore print

Fly Agaric

- Poisonous ☹
- Body emerges from soil looking like white eggs and turns red as it grows
- Small white to yellow pyramid-shaped warts

False Parasol

- Poisonous ☹
- White gills with no spores or green gills with green spores
- White to light brown stem

Jack O'Lantern

- Poisonous ☹
- Bright orange to yellowish
- Grows in clusters
- Cap convex
- Gills narrow
- Cream spore print

Destroying Angel

- Poisonous ☹
- White stalk and gills
- White cap or white edge and yellowish, pinkish, or tan center
- Egg-shaped cap

Shaggy Parasol

- Edible ☺
- Thick, fleshy scales on top of cap
- White spores
- White cap
- White gills
- Uniformly colored

Slippery Jack

- Edible ☺
- Brown cap, shiny and slimy when wet
- Dark chestnut brown
- Smooth semi-matt finish in summer

Spore Print

_____
_____
_____
_____
_____
_____

Location

Site / GPS: _____ Date: _____

○ Living Tree   ○ Leaf Litter   ○ Mulch   ○ Dead Tree or Wood   ○ Grass
○ Soil   ○ Other _____

Type of Tree(s) On or Near: _____

Forest Type: ○ Deciduous   ○ Coniferous   ○ Tropical   ○ Other _____

Weather Conditions: _____

General

Size (overall height): _____   Color: _____   Spore Color: _____

Texture: ○ Tough ○ Brittle ○ Leathery ○ Woody ○ Soft ○ Slimy
○ Spongy ○ Powdery ○ Waxy ○ Rubbery ○ Watery (Other) _____

Bruising When Touched? ○ Yes ○ No   Notes: _____

Structures: ○ Cup ○ Ring ○ Warts   _____

Cap Characteristics

Campanulate
(bell-shaped)

Conical
(triangular)

Cylindrical
(shaped like half an egg)

Convex
(outwardly rounded)

Flat
(with top of
uniform height)

Infundibuliform
(deeply, depressed,
funnel-shaped)

Depressed
(with a low
central region)

Umbonate
(with a central
bump or knob)

Surface Markings (warts, scales, slime, etc.): _____

Cap Margin: Smooth, Inrolled, Sinuous/Wavy, Other:_____

Color Changes: _____

Undercap

Gills ○

Attachment: Free or Decurrent

Spacing: Crowded, Close,
Distant, Subdistant

Color/Bruising: _____

Pores ○

Color: _____

Pore Size: _____

Pore Pattern: _____

Teeth ○

Color: _____

Teeth Length: _____

Flesh: Soft or Tough

○ Free
(gills not attached to stem)

○ Adnexed
(gills attached narrowly to stem)

○ Sinuate
(gills smoothly notched and running briefly down stem)

○ Adnate
(gills widely attached widely to stem)

○ Descenting
(gills running down stem for some length)

    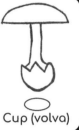

○ Tapering

○ Equal

○ Club-Shaped

○ Bulbous

○ Cup (volva)

Chanterelle

- Edible ☺
- Shape looks like bell of a trumpet
- Bright yellow/orange
- Similar look to Jack o'Lantern

Shaggy Mane

- Edible ☺
- White shaggy cylindrical cap that turns black and inky with age
- Bell shape when mature
- Spore print is black

Morels

- Edible ☺
- Honeycombed cap
- Most morels cap is longer than stem
- Spore print is usually light colored
- Interior is hollow

Puffballs

- Edible ☺
- Color is white
- Rounded-shaped balls with or without spiny warts on top
- Can be mistaken for golf ball, baseball or even soccer ball

Meadow Mushroom

- Edible ☺
- White or whitish
- Pink gills that turn brown with age
- Closely related to portobello

False Morel

- Poisonous ☹
- Red-brown cap is irregularly lobed, like a brain
- Hollow chambers inside the cap
- Yellowish spore print

Fly Agaric

- Poisonous ☹
- Body emerges from soil looking like white eggs and turns red as it grows
- Small white to yellow pyramid-shaped warts

False Parasol

- Poisonous ☹
- White gills with no spores or green gills with green spores
- White to light brown stem

Jack O'Lantern

- Poisonous ☹
- Bright orange to yellowish
- Grows in clusters
- Cap convex
- Gills narrow
- Cream spore print

Destroying Angel

- Poisonous ☹
- White stalk and gills
- White cap or white edge and yellowish, pinkish, or tan center
- Egg-shaped cap

Shaggy Parasol

- Edible ☺
- Thick, fleshy scales on top of cap
- White spores
- White cap
- White gills
- Uniformly colored

Slippery Jack

- Edible ☺
- Brown cap, shiny and slimy when wet
- Dark chestnut brown
- Smooth semi-matt finish in summer

Spore Print

_____
_____
_____
_____
_____
_____

Location

Site / GPS: _____ Date: _____

○ Living Tree ○ Leaf Litter ○ Mulch ○ Dead Tree or Wood ○ Grass
○ Soil ○ Other _____

Type of Tree(s) On or Near: _____

Forest Type: ○ Deciduous ○ Coniferous ○ Tropical ○ Other _____

Weather Conditions: _____

General

Size (overall height): _____ Color: _____ Spore Color: _____

Texture: ○ Tough ○ Brittle ○ Leathery ○ Woody ○ Soft ○ Slimy
○ Spongy ○ Powdery ○ Waxy ○ Rubbery ○ Watery (Other) _____

Bruising When Touched? ○ Yes ○ No   Notes: _____

Structures: ○ Cup ○ Ring ○ Warts   _____

Cap Characteristics

Campanulate
(bell-shaped)

Conical
(triangular)

Cylindrical
(shaped like half an egg)

Convex
(outwardly rounded)

Flat
(with top of
uniform height)

Infundibuliform
(deeply, depressed,
funnel-shaped)

Depressed
(with a low
central region)

Umbonate
(with a central
bump or knob)

Surface Markings (warts, scales, slime, etc.): _____

Cap Margin: Smooth, Inrolled, Sinuous/Wavy, Other: _____

Color Changes: _____

Undercap

Gills ○
Attachment: Free or Decurrent
Spacing: Crowded, Close,
Distant, Subdistant
Color/Bruising: _____

Pores ○
Color: _____
Pore Size: _____
Pore Pattern: _____

Teeth ○
Color: _____
Teeth Length: _____
Flesh: Soft or Tough

○ **Free**
(gills not attached to stem)

○ **Adnexed**
(gills attached narrowly to stem)

○ **Sinuate**
(gills smoothly notched and running briefly down stem)

○ **Adnate**
(gills widely attached widely to stem)

○ **Descenting**
(gills running down stem for some length)

   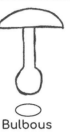 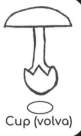

○ **Tapering** ○ **Equal** ○ **Club-Shaped** ○ **Bulbous** ○ **Cup (volva)**

Chanterelle
- Edible ☺
- Shape looks like bell of a trumpet
- Bright yellow/orange
- Similar look to Jack o'Lantern

Meadow Mushroom
- Edible ☺
- White or whitish
- Pink gills that turn brown with age
- Closely related to portobello

Jack O'Lantern
- Poisonous ☹
- Bright orange to yellowish
- Grows in clusters
- Cap convex
- Gills narrow
- Cream spore print

Shaggy Mane
- Edible ☺
- White shaggy cylindrical cap that turns black and inky with age
- Bell shape when mature
- Spore print is black

False Morel
- Poisonous ☹
- Red-brown cap is irregularly lobed, like a brain
- Hollow chambers inside the cap
- Yellowish spore print

Destroying Angel
- Poisonous ☹
- White stalk and gills
- White cap or white edge and yellowish, pinkish, or tan center
- Egg-shaped cap

Morels
- Edible ☺
- Honeycombed cap
- Most morels cap is longer than stem
- Spore print is usually light colored
- Interior is hollow

Fly Agaric
- Poisonous ☹
- Body emerges from soil looking like white eggs and turns red as it grows
- Small white to yellow pyramid-shaped warts

Shaggy Parasol
- Edible ☺
- Thick, fleshy scales on top of cap
- White spores
- White cap
- White gills
- Uniformly colored

Puffballs
- Edible ☺
- Color is white
- Rounded-shaped balls with or without spiny warts on top
- Can be mistaken for golf ball, baseball or even soccer ball

False Parasol
- Poisonous ☹
- White gills with no spores or green gills with green spores
- White to light brown stem

Slippery Jack
- Edible ☺
- Brown cap, shiny and slimy when wet
- Dark chestnut brown
- Smooth semi-matt finish in summer

Spore Print

_____

_____

_____

_____

_____

_____

Location

Site / GPS: _____ Date: _____

○ Living Tree ○ Leaf Litter ○ Mulch ○ Dead Tree or Wood ○ Grass
○ Soil ○ Other _____

Type of Tree(s) On or Near: _____

Forest Type: ○ Deciduous ○ Coniferous ○ Tropical ○ Other _____

Weather Conditions: _____

General

Size (overall height): _____ Color: _____ Spore Color: _____

Texture: ○ Tough ○ Brittle ○ Leathery ○ Woody ○ Soft ○ Slimy
○ Spongy ○ Powdery ○ Waxy ○ Rubbery ○ Watery (Other) _____

Bruising When Touched? ○ Yes ○ No Notes: _____

Structures: ○ Cup ○ Ring ○ Warts _____

Cap Characteristics

Campanulate
(bell-shaped)

Conical
(triangular)

Cylindrical
(shaped like half an egg)

Convex
(outwardly rounded)

Flat
(with top of
uniform height)

Infundibuliform
(deeply, depressed,
funnel-shaped)

Depressed
(with a low
central region)

Umbonate
(with a central
bump or knob)

Surface Markings (warts, scales, slime, etc.): _____

Cap Margin: Smooth, Inrolled, Sinuous/Wavy, Other:_____

Color Changes: _____

Undercap

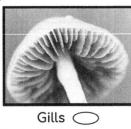

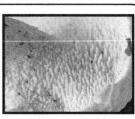

Gills ○

Attachment: Free or Decurrent

Spacing: Crowded, Close,
Distant, Subdistant

Color/Bruising: _____

Pores ○

Color: _____

Pore Size: _____

Pore Pattern: _____

Teeth ○

Color: _____

Teeth Length: _____

Flesh: Soft or Tough

◯ Free
(gills not attached to stem)

◯ Adnexed
(gills attached narrowly to stem)

◯ Sinuate
(gills smoothly notched and running briefly down stem)

◯ Adnate
(gills widely attached widely to stem)

◯ Descending
(gills running down stem for some length)

   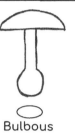 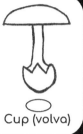

◯ Tapering

◯ Equal

◯ Club-Shaped

◯ Bulbous

◯ Cup (volva)

Chanterelle

- Edible ☺
- Shape looks like bell of a trumpet
- Bright yellow/orange
- Similar look to Jack o'Lantern

Meadow Mushroom

- Edible ☺
- White or whitish
- Pink gills that turn brown with age
- Closely related to portobello

Jack O'Lantern

- Poisonous ☹
- Bright orange to yellowish
- Grows in clusters
- Cap convex
- Gills narrow
- Cream spore print

Shaggy Mane

- Edible ☺
- White shaggy cylindrical cap that turns black and inky with age
- Bell shape when mature
- Spore print is black

False Morel

- Poisonous ☹
- Red-brown cap is irregularly lobed, like a brain
- Hollow chambers inside the cap
- Yellowish spore print

Destroying Angel

- Poisonous ☹
- White stalk and gills
- White cap or white edge and yellowish, pinkish, or tan center
- Egg-shaped cap

Morels

- Edible ☺
- Honeycombed cap
- Most morels cap is longer than stem
- Spore print is usually light colored
- Interior is hollow

Fly Agaric

- Poisonous ☹
- Body emerges from soil looking like white eggs and turns red as it grows
- Small white to yellow pyramid-shaped warts

Shaggy Parasol

- Edible ☺
- Thick, fleshy scales on top of cap
- White spores
- White cap
- White gills
- Uniformly colored

Puffballs

- Edible ☺
- Color is white
- Rounded-shaped balls with or without spiny warts on top
- Can be mistaken for golf ball, baseball or even soccer ball

False Parasol

- Poisonous ☹
- White gills with no spores or green gills with green spores
- White to light brown stem

Slippery Jack

- Edible ☺
- Brown cap, shiny and slimy when wet
- Dark chestnut brown
- Smooth semi-matt finish in summer

Spore Print

Location

Site / GPS: _____ Date: _____

◯ Living Tree ◯ Leaf Litter ◯ Mulch ◯ Dead Tree or Wood ◯ Grass
◯ Soil ◯ Other _____

Type of Tree(s) On or Near: _____

Forest Type: ◯ Deciduous ◯ Coniferous ◯ Tropical ◯ Other _____

Weather Conditions: _____

General

Size (overall height): _____ Color: _____ Spore Color: _____

Texture: ◯ Tough ◯ Brittle ◯ Leathery ◯ Woody ◯ Soft ◯ Slimy
◯ Spongy ◯ Powdery ◯ Waxy ◯ Rubbery ◯ Watery (Other) _____

Bruising When Touched? ◯ Yes ◯ No Notes: _____

Structures: ◯ Cup ◯ Ring ◯ Warts _____

Cap Characteristics

Campanulate
(bell-shaped)

Conical
(triangular)

Cylindrical
(shaped like half an egg)

Convex
(outwardly rounded)

Flat
(with top of
uniform height)

Infundibuliform
(deeply, depressed,
funnel-shaped)

Depressed
(with a low
central region)

Umbonate
(with a central
bump or knob)

Surface Markings (warts, scales, slime, etc.): _____

Cap Margin: Smooth, Inrolled, Sinuous/Wavy, Other: _____

Color Changes: _____

Undercap

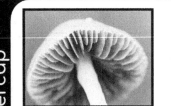

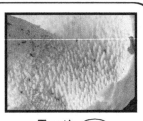

Gills ◯

Attachment: Free or Decurrent

Spacing: Crowded, Close,
Distant, Subdistant

Color/Bruising: _____

Pores ◯

Color: _____

Pore Size: _____

Pore Pattern: _____

Teeth ◯

Color: _____

Teeth Length: _____

Flesh: Soft or Tough

◯ **Free**
(gills not attached to stem)

◯ **Adnexed**
(gills attached narrowly to stem)

◯ **Sinuate**
(gills smoothly notched and running briefly down stem)

◯ **Adnate**
(gills widely attached widely to stem)

◯ **Descenting**
(gills running down stem for some length)

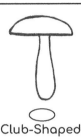

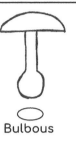

◯ **Tapering**

◯ **Equal**

◯ **Club-Shaped**

◯ **Bulbous**

◯ **Cup (volva)**

Chanterelle
- Edible ☺
- Shape looks like bell of a trumpet
- Bright yellow/orange
- Similar look to Jack o'Lantern

Meadow Mushroom
- Edible ☺
- White or whitish
- Pink gills that turn brown with age
- Closely related to portobello

Jack O'Lantern
- Poisonous ☹
- Bright orange to yellowish
- Grows in clusters
- Cap convex
- Gills narrow
- Cream spore print

Shaggy Mane
- Edible ☺
- White shaggy cylindrical cap that turns black and inky with age
- Bell shape when mature
- Spore print is black

False Morel
- Poisonous ☹
- Red-brown cap is irregularly lobed, like a brain
- Hollow chambers inside the cap
- Yellowish spore print

Destroying Angel
- Poisonous ☹
- White stalk and gills
- White cap or white edge and yellowish, pinkish, or tan center
- Egg-shaped cap

Morels
- Edible ☺
- Honeycombed cap
- Most morels cap is longer than stem
- Spore print is usually light colored
- Interior is hollow

Fly Agaric
- Poisonous ☹
- Body emerges from soil looking like white eggs and turns red as it grows
- Small white to yellow pyramid-shaped warts

Shaggy Parasol
- Edible ☺
- Thick, fleshy scales on top of cap
- White spores
- White cap
- White gills
- Uniformly colored

Puffballs
- Edible ☺
- Color is white
- Rounded-shaped balls with or without spiny warts on top
- Can be mistaken for golf ball, baseball or even soccer ball

False Parasol
- Poisonous ☹
- White gills with no spores or green gills with green spores
- White to light brown stem

Slippery Jack
- Edible ☺
- Brown cap, shiny and slimy when wet
- Dark chestnut brown
- Smooth semi-matt finish in summer

Spore Print

_____

_____

_____

_____

_____

_____

Location

Site / GPS: _____ Date: _____

○ Living Tree ○ Leaf Litter ○ Mulch ○ Dead Tree or Wood ○ Grass
○ Soil ○ Other _____

Type of Tree(s) On or Near: _____

Forest Type: ○ Deciduous ○ Coniferous ○ Tropical ○ Other _____

Weather Conditions: _____

General

Size (overall height): _____ Color: _____ Spore Color: _____

Texture: ○ Tough ○ Brittle ○ Leathery ○ Woody ○ Soft ○ Slimy
○ Spongy ○ Powdery ○ Waxy ○ Rubbery ○ Watery (Other) _____

Bruising When Touched? ○ Yes ○ No   Notes: _____

Structures: ○ Cup ○ Ring ○ Warts   _____

Cap Characteristics

Campanulate
(bell-shaped)

Conical
(triangular)

Cylindrical
(shaped like half an egg)

Convex
(outwardly rounded)

Flat
(with top of
uniform height)

Infundibuliform
(deeply, depressed,
funnel-shaped)

Depressed
(with a low
central region)

Umbonate
(with a central
bump or knob)

Surface Markings (warts, scales, slime, etc.): _____

Cap Margin: Smooth, Inrolled, Sinuous/Wavy, Other: _____

Color Changes: _____

Undercap

Gills ○
Attachment: Free or Decurrent
Spacing: Crowded, Close,
        Distant, Subdistant
Color/Bruising: _____

Pores ○
Color: _____
Pore Size: _____
Pore Pattern: _____

Teeth ○
Color: _____
Teeth Length: _____
Flesh: Soft or Tough

 ⬭ Free
(gills not attached
to stem)

⬭ Adnexed
(gills attached
narrowly to stem)

 ⬭ Sinuate
(gills smoothly notched
and running
briefly down stem)

 ⬭ Adnate
(gills widely attached
widely to stem)

 ⬭ Descenting
(gills running down
stem for some length)

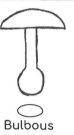

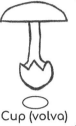

Tapering	Equal	Club-Shaped	Bulbous	Cup (volva)
⬭	⬭	⬭	⬭	⬭

Chanterelle

- Edible ☺
- Shape looks like bell of a trumpet
- Bright yellow/orange
- Similar look to Jack o'Lantern

Meadow Mushroom

- Edible ☺
- White or whitish
- Pink gills that turn brown with age
- Closely related to portobello

Jack O'Lantern

- Poisonous ☹
- Bright orange to yellowish
- Grows in clusters
- Cap convex
- Gills narrow
- Cream spore print

Shaggy Mane

- Edible ☺
- White shaggy cylindrical cap that turns black and inky with age
- Bell shape when mature
- Spore print is black

False Morel

- Poisonous ☹
- Red-brown cap is irregularly lobed, like a brain
- Hollow chambers inside the cap
- Yellowish spore print

Destroying Angel

- Poisonous ☹
- White stalk and gills
- White cap or white edge and yellowish, pinkish, or tan center
- Egg-shaped cap

Morels

- Edible ☺
- Honeycombed cap
- Most morels cap is longer than stem
- Spore print is usually light colored
- Interior is hollow

Fly Agaric

- Poisonous ☹
- Body emerges from soil looking like white eggs and turns red as it grows
- Small white to yellow pyramid-shaped warts

Shaggy Parasol

- Edible ☺
- Thick, fleshy scales on top of cap
- White spores
- White cap
- White gills
- Uniformly colored

Puffballs

- Edible ☺
- Color is white
- Rounded-shaped balls with or without spiny warts on top
- Can be mistaken for golf ball, baseball or even soccer ball

False Parasol

- Poisonous ☹
- White gills with no spores or green gills with green spores
- White to light brown stem

Slippery Jack

- Edible ☺
- Brown cap, shiny and slimy when wet
- Dark chestnut brown
- Smooth semi-matt finish in summer

Spore Print

Location

Site / GPS: _____ Date: _____

○ Living Tree ○ Leaf Litter ○ Mulch ○ Dead Tree or Wood ○ Grass
○ Soil ○ Other _____

Type of Tree(s) On or Near: _____

Forest Type: ○ Deciduous ○ Coniferous ○ Tropical ○ Other _____

Weather Conditions: _____

General

Size (overall height): _____ Color: _____ Spore Color: _____

Texture: ○ Tough ○ Brittle ○ Leathery ○ Woody ○ Soft ○ Slimy
○ Spongy ○ Powdery ○ Waxy ○ Rubbery ○ Watery (Other) _____

Bruising When Touched? ○ Yes ○ No Notes: _____

Structures: ○ Cup ○ Ring ○ Warts _____

Cap Characteristics

Campanulate
(bell-shaped)

Conical
(triangular)

Cylindrical
(shaped like half an egg)

Convex
(outwardly rounded)

Flat
(with top of uniform height)

Infundibuliform
(deeply, depressed, funnel-shaped)

Depressed
(with a low central region)

Umbonate
(with a central bump or knob)

Surface Markings (warts, scales, slime, etc.): _____

Cap Margin: Smooth, Inrolled, Sinuous/Wavy, Other: _____

Color Changes: _____

Undercap

Gills ○

Attachment: Free or Decurrent

Spacing: Crowded, Close, Distant, Subdistant

Color/Bruising: _____

Pores ○

Color: _____

Pore Size: _____

Pore Pattern: _____

Teeth ○

Color: _____

Teeth Length: _____

Flesh: Soft or Tough

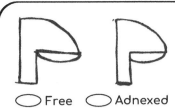

◯ Free
(gills not attached to stem)

◯ Adnexed
(gills attached narrowly to stem)

◯ Sinuate
(gills smoothly notched and running briefly down stem)

◯ Adnate
(gills widely attached widely to stem)

◯ Descenting
(gills running down stem for some length)

  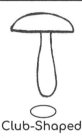 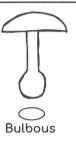 

◯ Tapering

◯ Equal

◯ Club-Shaped

◯ Bulbous

◯ Cup (volva)

Chanterelle
- Edible ☺
- Shape looks like bell of a trumpet
- Bright yellow/orange
- Similar look to Jack o'Lantern

Meadow Mushroom
- Edible ☺
- White or whitish
- Pink gills that turn brown with age
- Closely related to portobello

Jack O'Lantern
- Poisonous ☹
- Bright orange to yellowish
- Grows in clusters
- Cap convex
- Gills narrow
- Cream spore print

Shaggy Mane
- Edible ☺
- White shaggy cylindrical cap that turns black and inky with age
- Bell shape when mature
- Spore print is black

False Morel
- Poisonous ☹
- Red-brown cap is irregularly lobed, like a brain
- Hollow chambers inside the cap
- Yellowish spore print

Destroying Angel
- Poisonous ☹
- White stalk and gills
- White cap or white edge and yellowish, pinkish, or tan center
- Egg-shaped cap

Morels
- Edible ☺
- Honeycombed cap
- Most morels cap is longer than stem
- Spore print is usually light colored
- Interior is hollow

Fly Agaric
- Poisonous ☹
- Body emerges from soil looking like white eggs and turns red as it grows
- Small white to yellow pyramid-shaped warts

Shaggy Parasol
- Edible ☺
- Thick, fleshy scales on top of cap
- White spores
- White cap
- White gills
- Uniformly colored

Puffballs
- Edible ☺
- Color is white
- Rounded-shaped balls with or without spiny warts on top
- Can be mistaken for golf ball, baseball or even soccer ball

False Parasol
- Poisonous ☹
- White gills with no spores or green gills with green spores
- White to light brown stem

Slippery Jack
- Edible ☺
- Brown cap, shiny and slimy when wet
- Dark chestnut brown
- Smooth semi-matt finish in summer

Spore Print

_____
_____
_____
_____
_____
_____

Location

Site / GPS: _____ Date: _____

○ Living Tree ○ Leaf Litter ○ Mulch ○ Dead Tree or Wood ○ Grass
○ Soil ○ Other _____

Type of Tree(s) On or Near: _____

Forest Type: ○ Deciduous ○ Coniferous ○ Tropical ○ Other _____

Weather Conditions: _____

General

Size (overall height): _____ Color: _____ Spore Color: _____

Texture: ○ Tough ○ Brittle ○ Leathery ○ Woody ○ Soft ○ Slimy
○ Spongy ○ Powdery ○ Waxy ○ Rubbery ○ Watery (Other) _____

Bruising When Touched? ○ Yes ○ No   Notes: _____

Structures: ○ Cup ○ Ring ○ Warts   _____

Cap Characteristics

Campanulate
(bell-shaped)

Conical
(triangular)

Cylindrical
(shaped like half an egg)

Convex
(outwardly rounded)

Flat
(with top of
uniform height)

Infundibuliform
(deeply, depressed,
funnel-shaped)

Depressed
(with a low
central region)

Umbonate
(with a central
bump or knob)

Surface Markings (warts, scales, slime, etc.): _____

Cap Margin: Smooth, Inrolled, Sinuous/Wavy, Other:_____

Color Changes: _____

Undercap

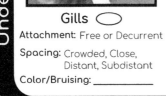

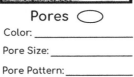

Gills ○

Attachment: Free or Decurrent

Spacing: Crowded, Close,
Distant, Subdistant

Color/Bruising: _____

Pores ○

Color: _____

Pore Size: _____

Pore Pattern: _____

Teeth ○

Color: _____

Teeth Length: _____

Flesh: Soft or Tough

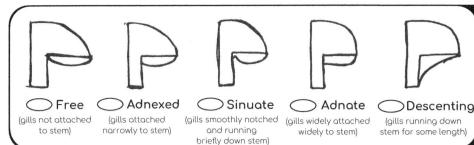

○ **Free**
(gills not attached to stem)

○ **Adnexed**
(gills attached narrowly to stem)

○ **Sinuate**
(gills smoothly notched and running briefly down stem)

○ **Adnate**
(gills widely attached widely to stem)

○ **Descenting**
(gills running down stem for some length)

  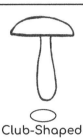 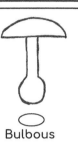 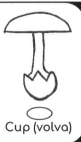

○ **Tapering**   ○ **Equal**   ○ **Club-Shaped**   ○ **Bulbous**   ○ **Cup (volva)**

Chanterelle
- Edible ☺
- Shape looks like bell of a trumpet
- Bright yellow/orange
- Similar look to Jack o'Lantern

Meadow Mushroom
- Edible ☺
- White or whitish
- Pink gills that turn brown with age
- Closely related to portobello

Jack O'Lantern
- Poisonous ☹
- Bright orange to yellowish
- Grows in clusters
- Cap convex
- Gills narrow
- Cream spore print

Shaggy Mane
- Edible ☺
- White shaggy cylindrical cap that turns black and inky with age
- Bell shape when mature
- Spore print is black

False Morel
- Poisonous ☹
- Red-brown cap is irregularly lobed, like a brain
- Hollow chambers inside the cap
- Yellowish spore print

Destroying Angel
- Poisonous ☹
- White stalk and gills
- White cap or white edge and yellowish, pinkish, or tan center
- Egg-shaped cap

Morels
- Edible ☺
- Honeycombed cap
- Most morels cap is longer than stem
- Spore print is usually light colored
- Interior is hollow

Fly Agaric
- Poisonous ☹
- Body emerges from soil looking like white eggs and turns red as it grows
- Small white to yellow pyramid-shaped warts

Shaggy Parasol
- Edible ☺
- Thick, fleshy scales on top of cap
- White spores
- White cap
- White gills
- Uniformly colored

Puffballs
- Edible ☺
- Color is white
- Rounded-shaped balls with or without spiny warts on top
- Can be mistaken for golf ball, baseball or even soccer ball

False Parasol
- Poisonous ☹
- White gills with no spores or green gills with green spores
- White to light brown stem

Slippery Jack
- Edible ☺
- Brown cap, shiny and slimy when wet
- Dark chestnut brown
- Smooth semi-matt finish in summer

Spore Print

_____
_____
_____
_____
_____
_____

Location

Site / GPS: _____ Date: _____

◯ Living Tree ◯ Leaf Litter ◯ Mulch ◯ Dead Tree or Wood ◯ Grass
◯ Soil ◯ Other _____

Type of Tree(s) On or Near: _____

Forest Type: ◯ Deciduous ◯ Coniferous ◯ Tropical ◯ Other _____

Weather Conditions: _____

General

Size (overall height): _____ Color: _____ Spore Color: _____

Texture: ◯ Tough ◯ Brittle ◯ Leathery ◯ Woody ◯ Soft ◯ Slimy
◯ Spongy ◯ Powdery ◯ Waxy ◯ Rubbery ◯ Watery (Other) _____

Bruising When Touched? ◯ Yes ◯ No Notes: _____

Structures: ◯ Cup ◯ Ring ◯ Warts _____

Cap Characteristics

Campanulate
(bell-shaped)

Conical
(triangular)

Cylindrical
(shaped like half an egg)

Convex
(outwardly rounded)

Flat
(with top of uniform height)

Infundibuliform
(deeply, depressed, funnel-shaped)

Depressed
(with a low central region)

Umbonate
(with a central bump or knob)

Surface Markings (warts, scales, slime, etc.): _____

Cap Margin: Smooth, Inrolled, Sinuous/Wavy, Other: _____

Color Changes: _____

Undercap

Gills ◯
Attachment: Free or Decurrent
Spacing: Crowded, Close, Distant, Subdistant
Color/Bruising: _____

Pores ◯
Color: _____
Pore Size: _____
Pore Pattern: _____

Teeth ◯
Color: _____
Teeth Length: _____
Flesh: Soft or Tough

○ Free
(gills not attached to stem)

○ Adnexed
(gills attached narrowly to stem)

○ Sinuate
(gills smoothly notched and running briefly down stem)

○ Adnate
(gills widely attached widely to stem)

○ Descending
(gills running down stem for some length)

Tapering

Equal

Club-Shaped

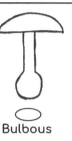

Bulbous

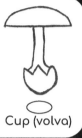

Cup (volva)

Chanterelle

- Edible ☺
- Shape looks like bell of a trumpet
- Bright yellow/orange
- Similar look to Jack o'Lantern

Meadow Mushroom

- Edible ☺
- White or whitish
- Pink gills that turn brown with age
- Closely related to portobello

Jack O'Lantern

- Poisonous ☹
- Bright orange to yellowish
- Grows in clusters
- Cap convex
- Gills narrow
- Cream spore print

Shaggy Mane

- Edible ☺
- White shaggy cylindrical cap that turns black and inky with age
- Bell shape when mature
- Spore print is black

False Morel

- Poisonous ☹
- Red-brown cap is irregularly lobed, like a brain
- Hollow chambers inside the cap
- Yellowish spore print

Destroying Angel

- Poisonous ☹
- White stalk and gills
- White cap or white edge and yellowish, pinkish, or tan center
- Egg-shaped cap

Morels

- Edible ☺
- Honeycombed cap
- Most morels cap is longer than stem
- Spore print is usually light colored
- Interior is hollow

Fly Agaric

- Poisonous ☹
- Body emerges from soil looking like white eggs and turns red as it grows
- Small white to yellow pyramid-shaped warts

Shaggy Parasol

- Edible ☺
- Thick, fleshy scales on top of cap
- White spores
- White cap
- White gills
- Uniformly colored

Puffballs

- Edible ☺
- Color is white
- Rounded-shaped balls with or without spiny warts on top
- Can be mistaken for golf ball, baseball or even soccer ball

False Parasol

- Poisonous ☹
- White gills with no spores or green gills with green spores
- White to light brown stem

Slippery Jack

- Edible ☺
- Brown cap, shiny and slimy when wet
- Dark chestnut brown
- Smooth semi-matt finish in summer

Spore Print

_____

_____

_____

_____

_____

_____

Location

Site / GPS: _____ Date: _____

○ Living Tree ○ Leaf Litter ○ Mulch ○ Dead Tree or Wood ○ Grass
○ Soil ○ Other _____

Type of Tree(s) On or Near: _____

Forest Type: ○ Deciduous ○ Coniferous ○ Tropical ○ Other _____

Weather Conditions: _____

General

Size (overall height): _____ Color: _____ Spore Color: _____

Texture: ○ Tough ○ Brittle ○ Leathery ○ Woody ○ Soft ○ Slimy
○ Spongy ○ Powdery ○ Waxy ○ Rubbery ○ Watery (Other) _____

Bruising When Touched? ○ Yes ○ No   Notes: _____

Structures: ○ Cup ○ Ring ○ Warts   _____

Cap Characteristics

Campanulate
(bell-shaped)

Conical
(triangular)

Cylindrical
(shaped like half an egg)

Convex
(outwardly rounded)

Flat
(with top of uniform height)

Infundibuliform
(deeply, depressed, funnel-shaped)

Depressed
(with a low central region)

Umbonate
(with a central bump or knob)

Surface Markings (warts, scales, slime, etc.): _____

Cap Margin: Smooth, Inrolled, Sinuous/Wavy, Other: _____

Color Changes: _____

Undercap

Gills ○
Attachment: Free or Decurrent
Spacing: Crowded, Close, Distant, Subdistant
Color/Bruising: _____

Pores ○
Color: _____
Pore Size: _____
Pore Pattern: _____

Teeth ○
Color: _____
Teeth Length: _____
Flesh: Soft or Tough

○ **Free**
(gills not attached to stem)

○ **Adnexed**
(gills attached narrowly to stem)

○ **Sinuate**
(gills smoothly notched and running briefly down stem)

○ **Adnate**
(gills widely attached widely to stem)

○ **Descenting**
(gills running down stem for some length)

   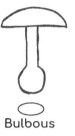 

○ **Tapering**   ○ **Equal**   ○ **Club-Shaped**   ○ **Bulbous**   ○ **Cup (volva)**

Chanterelle
- Edible ☺
- Shape looks like bell of a trumpet
- Bright yellow/orange
- Similar look to Jack o'Lantern

Meadow Mushroom
- Edible ☺
- White or whitish
- Pink gills that turn brown with age
- Closely related to portobello

Jack O'Lantern
- Poisonous ☹
- Bright orange to yellowish
- Grows in clusters
- Cap convex
- Gills narrow
- Cream spore print

Shaggy Mane
- Edible ☺
- White shaggy cylindrical cap that turns black and inky with age
- Bell shape when mature
- Spore print is black

False Morel
- Poisonous ☹
- Red-brown cap is irregularly lobed, like a brain
- Hollow chambers inside the cap
- Yellowish spore print

Destroying Angel
- Poisonous ☹
- White stalk and gills
- White cap or white edge and yellowish, pinkish, or tan center
- Egg-shaped cap

Morels
- Edible ☺
- Honeycombed cap
- Most morels cap is longer than stem
- Spore print is usually light colored
- Interior is hollow

Fly Agaric
- Poisonous ☹
- Body emerges from soil looking like white eggs and turns red as it grows
- Small white to yellow pyramid-shaped warts

Shaggy Parasol
- Edible ☺
- Thick, fleshy scales on top of cap
- White spores
- White cap
- White gills
- Uniformly colored

Puffballs
- Edible ☺
- Color is white
- Rounded-shaped balls with or without spiny warts on top
- Can be mistaken for golf ball, baseball or even soccer ball

False Parasol
- Poisonous ☹
- White gills with no spores or green gills with green spores
- White to light brown stem

Slippery Jack
- Edible ☺
- Brown cap, shiny and slimy when wet
- Dark chestnut brown
- Smooth semi-matt finish in summer

Spore Print

_____
_____
_____
_____
_____
_____

Location

Site / GPS: _____ Date: _____

○ Living Tree ○ Leaf Litter ○ Mulch ○ Dead Tree or Wood ○ Grass
○ Soil ○ Other _____

Type of Tree(s) On or Near: _____

Forest Type: ○ Deciduous ○ Coniferous ○ Tropical ○ Other _____

Weather Conditions: _____

General

Size (overall height): _____ Color: _____ Spore Color: _____

Texture: ○ Tough ○ Brittle ○ Leathery ○ Woody ○ Soft ○ Slimy
○ Spongy ○ Powdery ○ Waxy ○ Rubbery ○ Watery (Other) _____

Bruising When Touched? ○ Yes ○ No Notes: _____

Structures: ○ Cup ○ Ring ○ Warts _____

Cap Characteristics

Campanulate
(bell-shaped)

Conical
(triangular)

Cylindrical
(shaped like half an egg)

Convex
(outwardly rounded)

Flat
(with top of
uniform height)

Infundibuliform
(deeply, depressed,
funnel-shaped)

Depressed
(with a low
central region)

Umbonate
(with a central
bump or knob)

Surface Markings (warts, scales, slime, etc.): _____

Cap Margin: Smooth, Inrolled, Sinuous/Wavy, Other: _____

Color Changes: _____

Undercap

Gills ○

Attachment: Free or Decurrent

Spacing: Crowded, Close,
Distant, Subdistant

Color/Bruising: _____

Pores ○

Color: _____

Pore Size: _____

Pore Pattern: _____

Teeth ○

Color: _____

Teeth Length: _____

Flesh: Soft or Tough

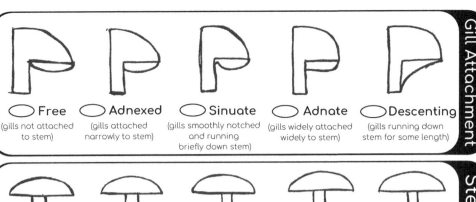

○ Free
(gills not attached to stem)

○ Adnexed
(gills attached narrowly to stem)

○ Sinuate
(gills smoothly notched and running briefly down stem)

○ Adnate
(gills widely attached widely to stem)

○ Descending
(gills running down stem for some length)

Tapering

Equal

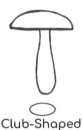
Club-Shaped

Bulbous

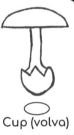
Cup (volva)

Chanterelle

- Edible ☺
- Shape looks like bell of a trumpet
- Bright yellow/orange
- Similar look to Jack o'Lantern

Shaggy Mane

- Edible ☺
- White shaggy cylindrical cap that turns black and inky with age
- Bell shape when mature
- Spore print is black

Morels

- Edible ☺
- Honeycombed cap
- Most morels cap is longer than stem
- Spore print is usually light colored
- Interior is hollow

Puffballs

- Edible ☺
- Color is white
- Rounded-shaped balls with or without spiny warts on top
- Can be mistaken for golf ball, baseball or even soccer ball

Meadow Mushroom

- Edible ☺
- White or whitish
- Pink gills that turn brown with age
- Closely related to portobello

False Morel

- Poisonous ☹
- Red-brown cap is irregularly lobed, like a brain
- Hollow chambers inside the cap
- Yellowish spore print

Fly Agaric

- Poisonous ☹
- Body emerges from soil looking like white eggs and turns red as it grows
- Small white to yellow pyramid-shaped warts

False Parasol

- Poisonous ☹
- White gills with no spores or green gills with green spores
- White to light brown stem

Jack O'Lantern

- Poisonous ☹
- Bright orange to yellowish
- Grows in clusters
- Cap convex
- Gills narrow
- Cream spore print

Destroying Angel

- Poisonous ☹
- White stalk and gills
- White cap or white edge and yellowish, pinkish, or tan center
- Egg-shaped cap

Shaggy Parasol

- Edible ☺
- Thick, fleshy scales on top of cap
- White spores
- White cap
- White gills
- Uniformly colored

Slippery Jack

- Edible ☺
- Brown cap, shiny and slimy when wet
- Dark chestnut brown
- Smooth semi-matt finish in summer

Spore Print

_____
_____
_____
_____
_____
_____

Location

Site / GPS: _____ Date: _____

◯ Living Tree ◯ Leaf Litter ◯ Mulch ◯ Dead Tree or Wood ◯ Grass
◯ Soil ◯ Other _____

Type of Tree(s) On or Near: _____

Forest Type: ◯ Deciduous ◯ Coniferous ◯ Tropical ◯ Other _____

Weather Conditions: _____

General

Size (overall height): _____ Color: _____ Spore Color: _____

Texture: ◯ Tough ◯ Brittle ◯ Leathery ◯ Woody ◯ Soft ◯ Slimy
◯ Spongy ◯ Powdery ◯ Waxy ◯ Rubbery ◯ Watery (Other) _____

Bruising When Touched? ◯ Yes ◯ No Notes: _____

Structures: ◯ Cup ◯ Ring ◯ Warts _____

Cap Characteristics

Campanulate
(bell-shaped)

Conical
(triangular)

Cylindrical
(shaped like half an egg)

Convex
(outwardly rounded)

Flat
(with top of
uniform height)

Infundibuliform
(deeply, depressed,
funnel-shaped)

Depressed
(with a low
central region)

Umbonate
(with a central
bump or knob)

Surface Markings (warts, scales, slime, etc.): _____

Cap Margin: Smooth, Inrolled, Sinuous/Wavy, Other: _____

Color Changes: _____

Undercap

Gills ◯

Attachment: Free or Decurrent

Spacing: Crowded, Close,
Distant, Subdistant

Color/Bruising: _____

Pores ◯

Color: _____

Pore Size: _____

Pore Pattern: _____

Teeth ◯

Color: _____

Teeth Length: _____

Flesh: Soft or Tough

   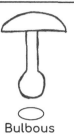 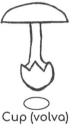

⬭ Free
(gills not attached to stem)

⬭ Adnexed
(gills attached narrowly to stem)

⬭ Sinuate
(gills smoothly notched and running briefly down stem)

⬭ Adnate
(gills widely attached widely to stem)

⬭ Descenting
(gills running down stem for some length)

⬭ Tapering   ⬭ Equal   ⬭ Club-Shaped   ⬭ Bulbous   ⬭ Cup (volva)

Chanterelle
- Edible ☺
- Shape looks like bell of a trumpet
- Bright yellow/orange
- Similar look to Jack o'Lantern

Shaggy Mane
- Edible ☺
- White shaggy cylindrical cap that turns black and inky with age
- Bell shape when mature
- Spore print is black

Morels
- Edible ☺
- Honeycombed cap
- Most morels cap is longer than stem
- Spore print is usually light colored
- Interior is hollow

Puffballs
- Edible ☺
- Color is white
- Rounded-shaped balls with or without spiny warts on top
- Can be mistaken for golf ball, baseball or even soccer ball

Meadow Mushroom
- Edible ☺
- White or whitish
- Pink gills that turn brown with age
- Closely related to portobello

False Morel
- Poisonous ☹
- Red-brown cap is irregularly lobed, like a brain
- Hollow chambers inside the cap
- Yellowish spore print

Fly Agaric
- Poisonous ☹
- Body emerges from soil looking like white eggs and turns red as it grows
- Small white to yellow pyramid-shaped warts

False Parasol
- Poisonous ☹
- White gills with no spores or green gills with green spores
- White to light brown stem

Jack O'Lantern
- Poisonous ☹
- Bright orange to yellowish
- Grows in clusters
- Cap convex
- Gills narrow
- Cream spore print

Destroying Angel
- Poisonous ☹
- White stalk and gills
- White cap or white edge and yellowish, pinkish, or tan center
- Egg-shaped cap

Shaggy Parasol
- Edible ☺
- Thick, fleshy scales on top of cap
- White spores
- White cap
- White gills
- Uniformly colored

Slippery Jack
- Edible ☺
- Brown cap, shiny and slimy when wet
- Dark chestnut brown
- Smooth semi-matt finish in summer

Spore Print

_____

_____

_____

_____

_____

_____

Location

Site / GPS: _____ Date: _____

◯ Living Tree ◯ Leaf Litter ◯ Mulch ◯ Dead Tree or Wood ◯ Grass
◯ Soil ◯ Other _____

Type of Tree(s) On or Near: _____

Forest Type: ◯ Deciduous ◯ Coniferous ◯ Tropical ◯ Other _____

Weather Conditions: _____

General

Size (overall height): _____ Color: _____ Spore Color: _____

Texture: ◯ Tough ◯ Brittle ◯ Leathery ◯ Woody ◯ Soft ◯ Slimy
◯ Spongy ◯ Powdery ◯ Waxy ◯ Rubbery ◯ Watery (Other) _____

Bruising When Touched? ◯ Yes ◯ No   Notes: _____

Structures: ◯ Cup ◯ Ring ◯ Warts   _____

Cap Characteristics

Campanulate
(bell-shaped)

Conical
(triangular)

Cylindrical
(shaped like half an egg)

Convex
(outwardly rounded)

Flat
(with top of
uniform height)

Infundibuliform
(deeply, depressed,
funnel-shaped)

Depressed
(with a low
central region)

Umbonate
(with a central
bump or knob)

Surface Markings (warts, scales, slime, etc.): _____

Cap Margin: Smooth, Inrolled, Sinuous/Wavy, Other: _____

Color Changes: _____

Undercap

Gills ◯
Attachment: Free or Decurrent
Spacing: Crowded, Close,
         Distant, Subdistant
Color/Bruising: _____

Pores ◯
Color: _____
Pore Size: _____
Pore Pattern: _____

Teeth ◯
Color: _____
Teeth Length: _____
Flesh: Soft or Tough

○ Free
(gills not attached to stem)

○ Adnexed
(gills attached narrowly to stem)

○ Sinuate
(gills smoothly notched and running briefly down stem)

○ Adnate
(gills widely attached widely to stem)

○ Descending
(gills running down stem for some length)

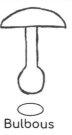
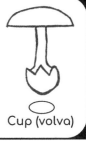

Tapering   **Equal**   **Club-Shaped**   **Bulbous**   **Cup (volva)**

Chanterelle

- Edible ☺
- Shape looks like bell of a trumpet
- Bright yellow/orange
- Similar look to Jack o'Lantern

Meadow Mushroom

- Edible ☺
- White or whitish
- Pink gills that turn brown with age
- Closely related to portobello

Jack O'Lantern

- Poisonous ☹
- Bright orange to yellowish
- Grows in clusters
- Cap convex
- Gills narrow
- Cream spore print

Shaggy Mane

- Edible ☺
- White shaggy cylindrical cap that turns black and inky with age
- Bell shape when mature
- Spore print is black

False Morel

- Poisonous ☹
- Red-brown cap is irregularly lobed, like a brain
- Hollow chambers inside the cap
- Yellowish spore print

Destroying Angel

- Poisonous ☹
- White stalk and gills
- White cap or white edge and yellowish, pinkish, or tan center
- Egg-shaped cap

Morels

- Edible ☺
- Honeycombed cap
- Most morels cap is longer than stem
- Spore print is usually light colored
- Interior is hollow

Fly Agaric

- Poisonous ☹
- Body emerges from soil looking like white eggs and turns red as it grows
- Small white to yellow pyramid-shaped warts

Shaggy Parasol

- Edible ☺
- Thick, fleshy scales on top of cap
- White spores
- White cap
- White gills
- Uniformly colored

Puffballs

- Edible ☺
- Color is white
- Rounded-shaped balls with or without spiny warts on top
- Can be mistaken for golf ball, baseball or even soccer ball

False Parasol

- Poisonous ☹
- White gills with no spores or green gills with green spores
- White to light brown stem

Slippery Jack

- Edible ☺
- Brown cap, shiny and slimy when wet
- Dark chestnut brown
- Smooth semi-matt finish in summer

Spore Print

_____
_____
_____
_____
_____
_____

Location

Site / GPS: _____ Date: _____

○ Living Tree ○ Leaf Litter ○ Mulch ○ Dead Tree or Wood ○ Grass
○ Soil ○ Other _____

Type of Tree(s) On or Near: _____

Forest Type: ○ Deciduous ○ Coniferous ○ Tropical ○ Other _____

Weather Conditions: _____

General

Size (overall height): _____ Color: _____ Spore Color: _____

Texture: ○ Tough ○ Brittle ○ Leathery ○ Woody ○ Soft ○ Slimy
○ Spongy ○ Powdery ○ Waxy ○ Rubbery ○ Watery (Other) _____

Bruising When Touched? ○ Yes ○ No   Notes: _____

Structures: ○ Cup ○ Ring ○ Warts   _____

Cap Characteristics

Campanulate
(bell-shaped)

Conical
(triangular)

Cylindrical
(shaped like half an egg)

Convex
(outwardly rounded)

Flat
(with top of
uniform height)

Infundibuliform
(deeply, depressed,
funnel-shaped)

Depressed
(with a low
central region)

Umbonate
(with a central
bump or knob)

Surface Markings (warts, scales, slime, etc.): _____

Cap Margin: Smooth, Inrolled, Sinuous/Wavy, Other: _____

Color Changes: _____

Undercap

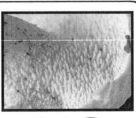

Gills ○

Attachment: Free or Decurrent

Spacing: Crowded, Close,
Distant, Subdistant

Color/Bruising: _____

Pores ○

Color: _____

Pore Size: _____

Pore Pattern: _____

Teeth ○

Color: _____

Teeth Length: _____

Flesh: Soft or Tough

◯ **Free**
(gills not attached to stem)

◯ **Adnexed**
(gills attached narrowly to stem)

◯ **Sinuate**
(gills smoothly notched and running briefly down stem)

◯ **Adnate**
(gills widely attached widely to stem)

◯ **Descenting**
(gills running down stem for some length)

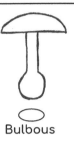

◯ **Tapering**

◯ **Equal**

◯ **Club-Shaped**

◯ **Bulbous**

◯ **Cup (volva)**

Chanterelle
- Edible ☺
- Shape looks like bell of a trumpet
- Bright yellow/orange
- Similar look to Jack o'Lantern

Shaggy Mane
- Edible ☺
- White shaggy cylindrical cap that turns black and inky with age
- Bell shape when mature
- Spore print is black

Morels
- Edible ☺
- Honeycombed cap
- Most morels cap is longer than stem
- Spore print is usually light colored
- Interior is hollow

Puffballs
- Edible ☺
- Color is white
- Rounded-shaped balls with or without spiny warts on top
- Can be mistaken for golf ball, baseball or even soccer ball

Meadow Mushroom
- Edible ☺
- White or whitish
- Pink gills that turn brown with age
- Closely related to portobello

False Morel
- Poisonous ☹
- Red-brown cap is irregularly lobed, like a brain
- Hollow chambers inside the cap
- Yellowish spore print

Fly Agaric
- Poisonous ☹
- Body emerges from soil looking like white eggs and turns red as it grows
- Small white to yellow pyramid-shaped warts

False Parasol
- Poisonous ☹
- White gills with no spores or green gills with green spores
- White to light brown stem

Jack O'Lantern
- Poisonous ☹
- Bright orange to yellowish
- Grows in clusters
- Cap convex
- Gills narrow
- Cream spore print

Destroying Angel
- Poisonous ☹
- White stalk and gills
- White cap or white edge and yellowish, pinkish, or tan center
- Egg-shaped cap

Shaggy Parasol
- Edible ☺
- Thick, fleshy scales on top of cap
- White spores
- White cap
- White gills
- Uniformly colored

Slippery Jack
- Edible ☺
- Brown cap, shiny and slimy when wet
- Dark chestnut brown
- Smooth semi-matt finish in summer

Spore Print

_____

_____

_____

_____

_____

_____

Location

Site / GPS: _____ Date: _____

○ Living Tree ○ Leaf Litter ○ Mulch ○ Dead Tree or Wood ○ Grass
○ Soil ○ Other _____

Type of Tree(s) On or Near: _____

Forest Type: ○ Deciduous ○ Coniferous ○ Tropical ○ Other _____

Weather Conditions: _____

General

Size (overall height): _____ Color: _____ Spore Color: _____

Texture: ○ Tough ○ Brittle ○ Leathery ○ Woody ○ Soft ○ Slimy
○ Spongy ○ Powdery ○ Waxy ○ Rubbery ○ Watery (Other) _____

Bruising When Touched? ○ Yes ○ No   Notes: _____

Structures: ○ Cup ○ Ring ○ Warts   _____

Cap Characteristics

Campanulate
(bell-shaped)

Conical
(triangular)

Cylindrical
(shaped like half an egg)

Convex
(outwardly rounded)

Flat
(with top of
uniform height)

Infundibuliform
(deeply, depressed,
funnel-shaped)

Depressed
(with a low
central region)

Umbonate
(with a central
bump or knob)

Surface Markings (warts, scales, slime, etc.): _____

Cap Margin: Smooth, Inrolled, Sinuous/Wavy, Other: _____

Color Changes: _____

Undercap

Gills ○

Attachment: Free or Decurrent

Spacing: Crowded, Close,
Distant, Subdistant

Color/Bruising: _____

Pores ○

Color: _____

Pore Size: _____

Pore Pattern: _____

Teeth ○

Color: _____

Teeth Length: _____

Flesh: Soft or Tough

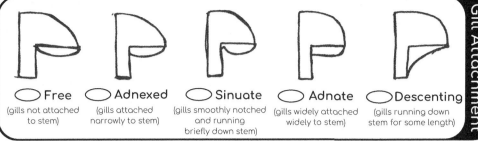

○ Free
(gills not attached to stem)

○ Adnexed
(gills attached narrowly to stem)

○ Sinuate
(gills smoothly notched and running briefly down stem)

○ Adnate
(gills widely attached widely to stem)

○ Descenting
(gills running down stem for some length)

   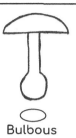 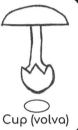

○ Tapering ○ Equal ○ Club-Shaped ○ Bulbous ○ Cup (volva)

Chanterelle

- Edible ☺
- Shape looks like bell of a trumpet
- Bright yellow/orange
- Similar look to Jack o'Lantern

Shaggy Mane

- Edible ☺
- White shaggy cylindrical cap that turns black and inky with age
- Bell shape when mature
- Spore print is black

Morels

- Edible ☺
- Honeycombed cap
- Most morels cap is longer than stem
- Spore print is usually light colored
- Interior is hollow

Puffballs

- Edible ☺
- Color is white
- Rounded-shaped balls with or without spiny warts on top
- Can be mistaken for golf ball, baseball or even soccer ball

Meadow Mushroom

- Edible ☺
- White or whitish
- Pink gills that turn brown with age
- Closely related to portobello

False Morel

- Poisonous ☹
- Red-brown cap is irregularly lobed, like a brain
- Hollow chambers inside the cap
- Yellowish spore print

Fly Agaric

- Poisonous ☹
- Body emerges from soil looking like white eggs and turns red as it grows
- Small white to yellow pyramid-shaped warts

False Parasol

- Poisonous ☹
- White gills with no spores or green gills with green spores
- White to light brown stem

Jack O'Lantern

- Poisonous ☹
- Bright orange to yellowish
- Grows in clusters
- Cap convex
- Gills narrow
- Cream spore print

Destroying Angel

- Poisonous ☹
- White stalk and gills
- White cap or white edge and yellowish, pinkish, or tan center
- Egg-shaped cap

Shaggy Parasol

- Edible ☺
- Thick, fleshy scales on top of cap
- White spores
- White cap
- White gills
- Uniformly colored

Slippery Jack

- Edible ☺
- Brown cap, shiny and slimy when wet
- Dark chestnut brown
- Smooth semi-matt finish in summer

Spore Print

_____

_____

_____

_____

_____

_____

Location

Site / GPS: _____ Date: _____

◯ Living Tree ◯ Leaf Litter ◯ Mulch ◯ Dead Tree or Wood ◯ Grass
◯ Soil ◯ Other _____

Type of Tree(s) On or Near: _____

Forest Type: ◯ Deciduous ◯ Coniferous ◯ Tropical ◯ Other _____

Weather Conditions: _____

General

Size (overall height): _____ Color: _____ Spore Color: _____

Texture: ◯ Tough ◯ Brittle ◯ Leathery ◯ Woody ◯ Soft ◯ Slimy
◯ Spongy ◯ Powdery ◯ Waxy ◯ Rubbery ◯ Watery (Other) _____

Bruising When Touched? ◯ Yes ◯ No Notes: _____

Structures: ◯ Cup ◯ Ring ◯ Warts _____

Cap Characteristics

Campanulate
(bell-shaped)

Conical
(triangular)

Cylindrical
(shaped like half an egg)

Convex
(outwardly rounded)

Flat
(with top of
uniform height)

Infundibuliform
(deeply, depressed,
funnel-shaped)

Depressed
(with a low
central region)

Umbonate
(with a central
bump or knob)

Surface Markings (warts, scales, slime, etc.): _____

Cap Margin: Smooth, Inrolled, Sinuous/Wavy, Other: _____

Color Changes: _____

Undercap

Gills ◯
Attachment: Free or Decurrent
Spacing: Crowded, Close,
Distant, Subdistant
Color/Bruising: _____

Pores ◯
Color: _____
Pore Size: _____
Pore Pattern: _____

Teeth ◯
Color: _____
Teeth Length: _____
Flesh: Soft or Tough

Free
(gills not attached to stem)

Adnexed
(gills attached narrowly to stem)

Sinuate
(gills smoothly notched and running briefly down stem)

Adnate
(gills widely attached widely to stem)

Descenting
(gills running down stem for some length)

  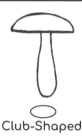 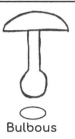 

Tapering

Equal

Club-Shaped

Bulbous

Cup (volva)

Chanterelle
- Edible ☺
- Shape looks like bell of a trumpet
- Bright yellow/orange
- Similar look to Jack o'Lantern

Shaggy Mane
- Edible ☺
- White shaggy cylindrical cap that turns black and inky with age
- Bell shape when mature
- Spore print is black

Morels
- Edible ☺
- Honeycombed cap
- Most morels cap is longer than stem
- Spore print is usually light colored
- Interior is hollow

Puffballs
- Edible ☺
- Color is white
- Rounded-shaped balls with or without spiny warts on top
- Can be mistaken for golf ball, baseball or even soccer ball

Meadow Mushroom
- Edible ☺
- White or whitish
- Pink gills that turn brown with age
- Closely related to portobello

False Morel
- Poisonous ☹
- Red-brown cap is irregularly lobed, like a brain
- Hollow chambers inside the cap
- Yellowish spore print

Fly Agaric
- Poisonous ☹
- Body emerges from soil looking like white eggs and turns red as it grows
- Small white to yellow pyramid-shaped warts

False Parasol
- Poisonous ☹
- White gills with no spores or green gills with green spores
- White to light brown stem

Jack O'Lantern
- Poisonous ☹
- Bright orange to yellowish
- Grows in clusters
- Cap convex
- Gills narrow
- Cream spore print

Destroying Angel
- Poisonous ☹
- White stalk and gills
- White cap or white edge and yellowish, pinkish, or tan center
- Egg-shaped cap

Shaggy Parasol
- Edible ☺
- Thick, fleshy scales on top of cap
- White spores
- White cap
- White gills
- Uniformly colored

Slippery Jack
- Edible ☺
- Brown cap, shiny and slimy when wet
- Dark chestnut brown
- Smooth semi-matt finish in summer

Spore Print

Location

Site / GPS: _____ Date: _____

○ Living Tree   ○ Leaf Litter   ○ Mulch   ○ Dead Tree or Wood   ○ Grass
○ Soil   ○ Other _____

Type of Tree(s) On or Near: _____

Forest Type: ○ Deciduous   ○ Coniferous   ○ Tropical   ○ Other _____

Weather Conditions: _____

General

Size (overall height): _____   Color: _____   Spore Color: _____

Texture: ○ Tough ○ Brittle ○ Leathery ○ Woody ○ Soft ○ Slimy
○ Spongy   ○ Powdery   ○ Waxy   ○ Rubbery   ○ Watery   (Other) _____

Bruising When Touched? ○ Yes ○ No   Notes: _____

Structures: ○ Cup ○ Ring ○ Warts   _____

Cap Characteristics

Campanulate
(bell-shaped)

Conical
(triangular)

Cylindrical
(shaped like half an egg)

Convex
(outwardly rounded)

Flat
(with top of
uniform height)

Infundibuliform
(deeply, depressed,
funnel-shaped)

Depressed
(with a low
central region)

Umbonate
(with a central
bump or knob)

Surface Markings (warts, scales, slime, etc.): _____

Cap Margin: Smooth, Inrolled, Sinuous/Wavy, Other: _____

Color Changes: _____

Undercap

Gills ○
Attachment: Free or Decurrent
Spacing: Crowded, Close,
        Distant, Subdistant
Color/Bruising: _____

Pores ○
Color: _____
Pore Size: _____
Pore Pattern: _____

Teeth ○
Color: _____
Teeth Length: _____
Flesh: Soft or Tough

○ **Free**
(gills not attached to stem)

○ **Adnexed**
(gills attached narrowly to stem)

○ **Sinuate**
(gills smoothly notched and running briefly down stem)

○ **Adnate**
(gills widely attached widely to stem)

○ **Descenting**
(gills running down stem for some length)

  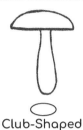 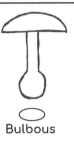 

○ **Tapering**   ○ **Equal**   ○ **Club-Shaped**   ○ **Bulbous**   ○ **Cup (volva)**

Chanterelle
- Edible ☺
- Shape looks like bell of a trumpet
- Bright yellow/orange
- Similar look to Jack o'Lantern

Meadow Mushroom
- Edible ☺
- White or whitish
- Pink gills that turn brown with age
- Closely related to portobello

Jack O'Lantern
- Poisonous ☹
- Bright orange to yellowish
- Grows in clusters
- Cap convex
- Gills narrow
- Cream spore print

Shaggy Mane
- Edible ☺
- White shaggy cylindrical cap that turns black and inky with age
- Bell shape when mature
- Spore print is black

False Morel
- Poisonous ☹
- Red-brown cap is irregularly lobed, like a brain
- Hollow chambers inside the cap
- Yellowish spore print

Destroying Angel
- Poisonous ☹
- White stalk and gills
- White cap or white edge and yellowish, pinkish, or tan center
- Egg-shaped cap

Morels
- Edible ☺
- Honeycombed cap
- Most morels cap is longer than stem
- Spore print is usually light colored
- Interior is hollow

Fly Agaric
- Poisonous ☹
- Body emerges from soil looking like white eggs and turns red as it grows
- Small white to yellow pyramid-shaped warts

Shaggy Parasol
- Edible ☺
- Thick, fleshy scales on top of cap
- White spores
- White cap
- White gills
- Uniformly colored

Puffballs
- Edible ☺
- Color is white
- Rounded-shaped balls with or without spiny warts on top
- Can be mistaken for golf ball, baseball or even soccer ball

False Parasol
- Poisonous ☹
- White gills with no spores or green gills with green spores
- White to light brown stem

Slippery Jack
- Edible ☺
- Brown cap, shiny and slimy when wet
- Dark chestnut brown
- Smooth semi-matt finish in summer

Spore Print

_____
_____
_____
_____
_____
_____

Location

Site / GPS: _____ Date: _____

◯ Living Tree ◯ Leaf Litter ◯ Mulch ◯ Dead Tree or Wood ◯ Grass
◯ Soil ◯ Other _____

Type of Tree(s) On or Near: _____

Forest Type: ◯ Deciduous ◯ Coniferous ◯ Tropical ◯ Other _____

Weather Conditions: _____

General

Size (overall height): _____ Color: _____ Spore Color: _____

Texture: ◯ Tough ◯ Brittle ◯ Leathery ◯ Woody ◯ Soft ◯ Slimy
◯ Spongy ◯ Powdery ◯ Waxy ◯ Rubbery ◯ Watery (Other) _____
Bruising When Touched? ◯ Yes ◯ No Notes: _____
Structures: ◯ Cup ◯ Ring ◯ Warts _____

Cap Characteristics

Campanulate
(bell-shaped)

Conical
(triangular)

Cylindrical
(shaped like half an egg)

Convex
(outwardly rounded)

Flat
(with top of
uniform height)

Infundibuliform
(deeply, depressed,
funnel-shaped)

Depressed
(with a low
central region)

Umbonate
(with a central
bump or knob)

Surface Markings (warts, scales, slime, etc.): _____

Cap Margin: Smooth, Inrolled, Sinuous/Wavy, Other: _____

Color Changes: _____

Undercap

Gills ◯

Attachment: Free or Decurrent

Spacing: Crowded, Close,
Distant, Subdistant

Color/Bruising: _____

Pores ◯

Color: _____

Pore Size: _____

Pore Pattern: _____

Teeth ◯

Color: _____

Teeth Length: _____

Flesh: Soft or Tough

Free	Adnexed	Sinuate	Adnate	Descending
(gills not attached to stem)	(gills attached narrowly to stem)	(gills smoothly notched and running briefly down stem)	(gills widely attached widely to stem)	(gills running down stem for some length)

   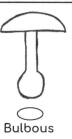 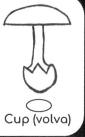

Tapering	Equal	Club-Shaped	Bulbous	Cup (volva)

Chanterelle
- Edible ☺
- Shape looks like bell of a trumpet
- Bright yellow/orange
- Similar look to Jack o'Lantern

Shaggy Mane
- Edible ☺
- White shaggy cylindrical cap that turns black and inky with age
- Bell shape when mature
- Spore print is black

Morels
- Edible ☺
- Honeycombed cap
- Most morels cap is longer than stem
- Spore print is usually light colored
- Interior is hollow

Puffballs
- Edible ☺
- Color is white
- Rounded-shaped balls with or without spiny warts on top
- Can be mistaken for golf ball, baseball or even soccer ball

Meadow Mushroom
- Edible ☺
- White or whitish
- Pink gills that turn brown with age
- Closely related to portobello

False Morel
- Poisonous ☹
- Red-brown cap is irregularly lobed, like a brain
- Hollow chambers inside the cap
- Yellowish spore print

Fly Agaric
- Poisonous ☹
- Body emerges from soil looking like white eggs and turns red as it grows
- Small white to yellow pyramid-shaped warts

False Parasol
- Poisonous ☹
- White gills with no spores or green gills with green spores
- White to light brown stem

Jack O'Lantern
- Poisonous ☹
- Bright orange to yellowish
- Grows in clusters
- Cap convex
- Gills narrow
- Cream spore print

Destroying Angel
- Poisonous ☹
- White stalk and gills
- White cap or white edge and yellowish, pinkish, or tan center
- Egg-shaped cap

Shaggy Parasol
- Edible ☺
- Thick, fleshy scales on top of cap
- White spores
- White cap
- White gills
- Uniformly colored

Slippery Jack
- Edible ☺
- Brown cap, shiny and slimy when wet
- Dark chestnut brown
- Smooth semi-matt finish in summer

Spore Print

_____
_____
_____
_____
_____
_____

Location

Site / GPS: _____ Date: _____

○ Living Tree ○ Leaf Litter ○ Mulch ○ Dead Tree or Wood ○ Grass
○ Soil ○ Other _____

Type of Tree(s) On or Near: _____

Forest Type: ○ Deciduous ○ Coniferous ○ Tropical ○ Other _____

Weather Conditions: _____

General

Size (overall height): _____ Color: _____ Spore Color: _____

Texture: ○ Tough ○ Brittle ○ Leathery ○ Woody ○ Soft ○ Slimy
○ Spongy ○ Powdery ○ Waxy ○ Rubbery ○ Watery (Other) _____

Bruising When Touched? ○ Yes ○ No   Notes: _____

Structures: ○ Cup ○ Ring ○ Warts   _____

Cap Characteristics

Campanulate
(bell-shaped)

Conical
(triangular)

Cylindrical
(shaped like half an egg)

Convex
(outwardly rounded)

Flat
(with top of
uniform height)

Infundibuliform
(deeply, depressed,
funnel-shaped)

Depressed
(with a low
central region)

Umbonate
(with a central
bump or knob)

Surface Markings (warts, scales, slime, etc.): _____

Cap Margin: Smooth, Inrolled, Sinuous/Wavy, Other:_____

Color Changes: _____

Undercap

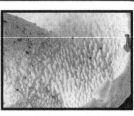

Gills ○

Attachment: Free or Decurrent

Spacing: Crowded, Close,
Distant, Subdistant

Color/Bruising: _____

Pores ○

Color: _____

Pore Size: _____

Pore Pattern: _____

Teeth ○

Color: _____

Teeth Length: _____

Flesh: Soft or Tough

 Free
(gills not attached to stem)

Adnexed
(gills attached narrowly to stem)

Sinuate
(gills smoothly notched and running briefly down stem)

Adnate
(gills widely attached widely to stem)

Descenting
(gills running down stem for some length)

  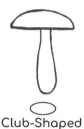 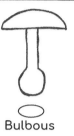 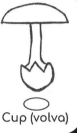

Tapering Equal Club-Shaped Bulbous Cup (volva)

Chanterelle
- Edible ☺
- Shape looks like bell of a trumpet
- Bright yellow/orange
- Similar look to Jack o'Lantern

Meadow Mushroom
- Edible ☺
- White or whitish
- Pink gills that turn brown with age
- Closely related to portobello

Jack O'Lantern
- Poisonous ☹
- Bright orange to yellowish
- Grows in clusters
- Cap convex
- Gills narrow
- Cream spore print

Shaggy Mane
- Edible ☺
- White shaggy cylindrical cap that turns black and inky with age
- Bell shape when mature
- Spore print is black

False Morel
- Poisonous ☹
- Red-brown cap is irregularly lobed, like a brain
- Hollow chambers inside the cap
- Yellowish spore print

Destroying Angel
- Poisonous ☹
- White stalk and gills
- White cap or white edge and yellowish, pinkish, or tan center
- Egg-shaped cap

Morels
- Edible ☺
- Honeycombed cap
- Most morels cap is longer than stem
- Spore print is usually light colored
- Interior is hollow

Fly Agaric
- Poisonous ☹
- Body emerges from soil looking like white eggs and turns red as it grows
- Small white to yellow pyramid-shaped warts

Shaggy Parasol
- Edible ☺
- Thick, fleshy scales on top of cap
- White spores
- White cap
- White gills
- Uniformly colored

Puffballs
- Edible ☺
- Color is white
- Rounded-shaped balls with or without spiny warts on top
- Can be mistaken for golf ball, baseball or even soccer ball

False Parasol
- Poisonous ☹
- White gills with no spores or green gills with green spores
- White to light brown stem

Slippery Jack
- Edible ☺
- Brown cap, shiny and slimy when wet
- Dark chestnut brown
- Smooth semi-matt finish in summer

Spore Print

_____
_____
_____
_____
_____
_____

Location

Site / GPS: _____ Date: _____

○ Living Tree ○ Leaf Litter ○ Mulch ○ Dead Tree or Wood ○ Grass
○ Soil ○ Other _____

Type of Tree(s) On or Near: _____

Forest Type: ○ Deciduous ○ Coniferous ○ Tropical ○ Other _____

Weather Conditions: _____

General

Size (overall height): _____ Color: _____ Spore Color: _____

Texture: ○ Tough ○ Brittle ○ Leathery ○ Woody ○ Soft ○ Slimy
○ Spongy ○ Powdery ○ Waxy ○ Rubbery ○ Watery (Other) _____

Bruising When Touched? ○ Yes ○ No Notes: _____

Structures: ○ Cup ○ Ring ○ Warts _____

Cap Characteristics

Campanulate
(bell-shaped)

Conical
(triangular)

Cylindrical
(shaped like half an egg)

Convex
(outwardly rounded)

Flat
(with top of
uniform height)

Infundibuliform
(deeply, depressed,
funnel-shaped)

Depressed
(with a low
central region)

Umbonate
(with a central
bump or knob)

Surface Markings (warts, scales, slime, etc.): _____

Cap Margin: Smooth, Inrolled, Sinuous/Wavy, Other:_____

Color Changes: _____

Undercap

Gills ○
Attachment: Free or Decurrent
Spacing: Crowded, Close,
       Distant, Subdistant
Color/Bruising: _____

Pores ○
Color: _____
Pore Size: _____
Pore Pattern: _____

Teeth ○
Color: _____
Teeth Length: _____
Flesh: Soft or Tough

○ Free
(gills not attached to stem)

○ Adnexed
(gills attached narrowly to stem)

○ Sinuate
(gills smoothly notched and running briefly down stem)

○ Adnate
(gills widely attached widely to stem)

○ Descenting
(gills running down stem for some length)

○ Tapering

○ Equal

○ Club-Shaped

○ Bulbous

○ Cup (volva)

Chanterelle
- Edible ☺
- Shape looks like bell of a trumpet
- Bright yellow/orange
- Similar look to Jack o'Lantern

Shaggy Mane
- Edible ☺
- White shaggy cylindrical cap that turns black and inky with age
- Bell shape when mature
- Spore print is black

Morels
- Edible ☺
- Honeycombed cap
- Most morels cap is longer than stem
- Spore print is usually light colored
- Interior is hollow

Puffballs
- Edible ☺
- Color is white
- Rounded-shaped balls with or without spiny warts on top
- Can be mistaken for golf ball, baseball or even soccer ball

Meadow Mushroom
- Edible ☺
- White or whitish
- Pink gills that turn brown with age
- Closely related to portobello

False Morel
- Poisonous ☹
- Red-brown cap is irregularly lobed, like a brain
- Hollow chambers inside the cap
- Yellowish spore print

Fly Agaric
- Poisonous ☹
- Body emerges from soil looking like white eggs and turns red as it grows
- Small white to yellow pyramid-shaped warts

False Parasol
- Poisonous ☹
- White gills with no spores or green gills with green spores
- White to light brown stem

Jack O'Lantern
- Poisonous ☹
- Bright orange to yellowish
- Grows in clusters
- Cap convex
- Gills narrow
- Cream spore print

Destroying Angel
- Poisonous ☹
- White stalk and gills
- White cap or white edge and yellowish, pinkish, or tan center
- Egg-shaped cap

Shaggy Parasol
- Edible ☺
- Thick, fleshy scales on top of cap
- White spores
- White cap
- White gills
- Uniformly colored

Slippery Jack
- Edible ☺
- Brown cap, shiny and slimy when wet
- Dark chestnut brown
- Smooth semi-matt finish in summer

Spore Print

_____
_____
_____
_____
_____
_____

Location

Site / GPS: _____ Date: _____

◯ Living Tree   ◯ Leaf Litter   ◯ Mulch   ◯ Dead Tree or Wood   ◯ Grass
◯ Soil   ◯ Other _____

Type of Tree(s) On or Near: _____

Forest Type: ◯ Deciduous   ◯ Coniferous   ◯ Tropical   ◯ Other _____

Weather Conditions: _____

General

Size (overall height): _____ Color: _____ Spore Color: _____

Texture: ◯ Tough ◯ Brittle ◯ Leathery ◯ Woody ◯ Soft ◯ Slimy
◯ Spongy ◯ Powdery ◯ Waxy ◯ Rubbery ◯ Watery (Other) _____

Bruising When Touched? ◯ Yes ◯ No   Notes: _____

Structures: ◯ Cup ◯ Ring ◯ Warts   _____

Cap Characteristics

Campanulate
(bell-shaped)

Conical
(triangular)

Cylindrical
(shaped like half an egg)

Convex
(outwardly rounded)

Flat
(with top of
uniform height)

Infundibuliform
(deeply, depressed,
funnel-shaped)

Depressed
(with a low
central region)

Umbonate
(with a central
bump or knob)

Surface Markings (warts, scales, slime, etc.): _____

Cap Margin: Smooth, Inrolled, Sinuous/Wavy, Other:_____

Color Changes: _____

Undercap

Gills ◯
Attachment: Free or Decurrent
Spacing: Crowded, Close,
         Distant, Subdistant
Color/Bruising: _____

Pores ◯
Color: _____
Pore Size: _____
Pore Pattern:_____

Teeth ◯
Color: _____
Teeth Length: _____
Flesh: Soft or Tough

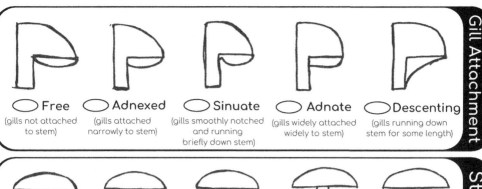

○ **Free**
(gills not attached to stem)

○ **Adnexed**
(gills attached narrowly to stem)

○ **Sinuate**
(gills smoothly notched and running briefly down stem)

○ **Adnate**
(gills widely attached widely to stem)

○ **Descenting**
(gills running down stem for some length)

  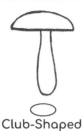  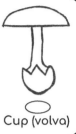

○ **Tapering**   ○ **Equal**   ○ **Club-Shaped**   ○ **Bulbous**   ○ **Cup (volva)**

Chanterelle
- Edible ☺
- Shape looks like bell of a trumpet
- Bright yellow/orange
- Similar look to Jack o'Lantern

Meadow Mushroom
- Edible ☺
- White or whitish
- Pink gills that turn brown with age
- Closely related to portobello

Jack O'Lantern
- Poisonous ☹
- Bright orange to yellowish
- Grows in clusters
- Cap convex
- Gills narrow
- Cream spore print

Shaggy Mane
- Edible ☺
- White shaggy cylindrical cap that turns black and inky with age
- Bell shape when mature
- Spore print is black

False Morel
- Poisonous ☹
- Red-brown cap is irregularly lobed, like a brain
- Hollow chambers inside the cap
- Yellowish spore print

Destroying Angel
- Poisonous ☹
- White stalk and gills
- White cap or white edge and yellowish, pinkish, or tan center
- Egg-shaped cap

Morels
- Edible ☺
- Honeycombed cap
- Most morels cap is longer than stem
- Spore print is usually light colored
- Interior is hollow

Fly Agaric
- Poisonous ☹
- Body emerges from soil looking like white eggs and turns red as it grows
- Small white to yellow pyramid-shaped warts

Shaggy Parasol
- Edible ☺
- Thick, fleshy scales on top of cap
- White spores
- White cap
- White gills
- Uniformly colored

Puffballs
- Edible ☺
- Color is white
- Rounded-shaped balls with or without spiny warts on top
- Can be mistaken for golf ball, baseball or even soccer ball

False Parasol
- Poisonous ☹
- White gills with no spores or green gills with green spores
- White to light brown stem

Slippery Jack
- Edible ☺
- Brown cap, shiny and slimy when wet
- Dark chestnut brown
- Smooth semi-matt finish in summer

Spore Print

_____
_____
_____
_____
_____
_____

Location

Site / GPS: _____ Date: _____

○ Living Tree   ○ Leaf Litter   ○ Mulch   ○ Dead Tree or Wood   ○ Grass
○ Soil   ○ Other _____

Type of Tree(s) On or Near: _____

Forest Type: ○ Deciduous   ○ Coniferous   ○ Tropical   ○ Other _____

Weather Conditions: _____

General

Size (overall height): _____   Color: _____   Spore Color: _____

Texture: ○ Tough ○ Brittle ○ Leathery ○ Woody ○ Soft ○ Slimy
○ Spongy ○ Powdery ○ Waxy ○ Rubbery ○ Watery (Other) _____

Bruising When Touched? ○ Yes ○ No   Notes: _____

Structures: ○ Cup ○ Ring ○ Warts   _____

Cap Characteristics

Campanulate
(bell-shaped)

Conical
(triangular)

Cylindrical
(shaped like half an egg)

Convex
(outwardly rounded)

Flat
(with top of
uniform height)

Infundibuliform
(deeply, depressed,
funnel-shaped)

Depressed
(with a low
central region)

Umbonate
(with a central
bump or knob)

Surface Markings (warts, scales, slime, etc.): _____

Cap Margin: Smooth, Inrolled, Sinuous/Wavy, Other: _____

Color Changes: _____

Undercap

Gills ○
Attachment: Free or Decurrent
Spacing: Crowded, Close,
       Distant, Subdistant
Color/Bruising: _____

Pores ○
Color: _____
Pore Size: _____
Pore Pattern: _____

Teeth ○
Color: _____
Teeth Length: _____
Flesh: Soft or Tough

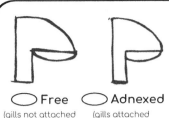

○ Free
(gills not attached to stem)

○ Adnexed
(gills attached narrowly to stem)

○ Sinuate
(gills smoothly notched and running briefly down stem)

○ Adnate
(gills widely attached widely to stem)

○ Descending
(gills running down stem for some length)

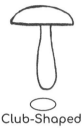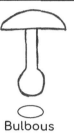

○ Tapering

○ Equal

○ Club-Shaped

○ Bulbous

○ Cup (volva)

Chanterelle
- Edible ☺
- Shape looks like bell of a trumpet
- Bright yellow/orange
- Similar look to Jack o'Lantern

Meadow Mushroom
- Edible ☺
- White or whitish
- Pink gills that turn brown with age
- Closely related to portobello

Jack O'Lantern
- Poisonous ☹
- Bright orange to yellowish
- Grows in clusters
- Cap convex
- Gills narrow
- Cream spore print

Shaggy Mane
- Edible ☺
- White shaggy cylindrical cap that turns black and inky with age
- Bell shape when mature
- Spore print is black

False Morel
- Poisonous ☹
- Red-brown cap is irregularly lobed, like a brain
- Hollow chambers inside the cap
- Yellowish spore print

Destroying Angel
- Poisonous ☹
- White stalk and gills
- White cap or white edge and yellowish, pinkish, or tan center
- Egg-shaped cap

Morels
- Edible ☺
- Honeycombed cap
- Most morels cap is longer than stem
- Spore print is usually light colored
- Interior is hollow

Fly Agaric
- Poisonous ☹
- Body emerges from soil looking like white eggs and turns red as it grows
- Small white to yellow pyramid-shaped warts

Shaggy Parasol
- Edible ☺
- Thick, fleshy scales on top of cap
- White spores
- White cap
- White gills
- Uniformly colored

Puffballs
- Edible ☺
- Color is white
- Rounded-shaped balls with or without spiny warts on top
- Can be mistaken for golf ball, baseball or even soccer ball

False Parasol
- Poisonous ☹
- White gills with no spores or green gills with green spores
- White to light brown stem

Slippery Jack
- Edible ☺
- Brown cap, shiny and slimy when wet
- Dark chestnut brown
- Smooth semi-matt finish in summer

Spore Print

Location

Site / GPS: _____ Date: _____

○ Living Tree ○ Leaf Litter ○ Mulch ○ Dead Tree or Wood ○ Grass

○ Soil ○ Other _____

Type of Tree(s) On or Near: _____

Forest Type: ○ Deciduous ○ Coniferous ○ Tropical ○ Other _____

Weather Conditions: _____

General

Size (overall height): _____ Color: _____ Spore Color: _____

Texture: ○ Tough ○ Brittle ○ Leathery ○ Woody ○ Soft ○ Slimy

○ Spongy ○ Powdery ○ Waxy ○ Rubbery ○ Watery (Other) _____

Bruising When Touched? ○ Yes ○ No Notes: _____

Structures: ○ Cup ○ Ring ○ Warts _____

Cap Characteristics

Campanulate
(bell-shaped)

Conical
(triangular)

Cylindrical
(shaped like half an egg)

Convex
(outwardly rounded)

Flat
(with top of
uniform height)

Infundibuliform
(deeply, depressed,
funnel-shaped)

Depressed
(with a low
central region)

Umbonate
(with a central
bump or knob)

Surface Markings (warts, scales, slime, etc.): _____

Cap Margin: Smooth, Inrolled, Sinuous/Wavy, Other: _____

Color Changes: _____

Undercap

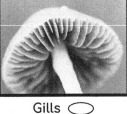

Gills ○

Attachment: Free or Decurrent

Spacing: Crowded, Close,
Distant, Subdistant

Color/Bruising: _____

Pores ○

Color: _____

Pore Size: _____

Pore Pattern: _____

Teeth ○

Color: _____

Teeth Length: _____

Flesh: Soft or Tough

 Free
(gills not attached to stem)

 Adnexed
(gills attached narrowly to stem)

 Sinuate
(gills smoothly notched and running briefly down stem)

 Adnate
(gills widely attached widely to stem)

 Descenting
(gills running down stem for some length)

Tapering

Equal

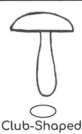

Club-Shaped

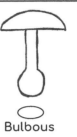

Bulbous

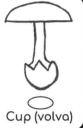

Cup (volva)

Chanterelle

- Edible ☺
- Shape looks like bell of a trumpet
- Bright yellow/orange
- Similar look to Jack o'Lantern

Meadow Mushroom

- Edible ☺
- White or whitish
- Pink gills that turn brown with age
- Closely related to portobello

Jack O'Lantern

- Poisonous ☹
- Bright orange to yellowish
- Grows in clusters
- Cap convex
- Gills narrow
- Cream spore print

Shaggy Mane

- Edible ☺
- White shaggy cylindrical cap that turns black and inky with age
- Bell shape when mature
- Spore print is black

False Morel

- Poisonous ☹
- Red-brown cap is irregularly lobed, like a brain
- Hollow chambers inside the cap
- Yellowish spore print

Destroying Angel

- Poisonous ☹
- White stalk and gills
- White cap or white edge and yellowish, pinkish, or tan center
- Egg-shaped cap

Morels

- Edible ☺
- Honeycombed cap
- Most morels cap is longer than stem
- Spore print is usually light colored
- Interior is hollow

Fly Agaric

- Poisonous ☹
- Body emerges from soil looking like white eggs and turns red as it grows
- Small white to yellow pyramid-shaped warts

Shaggy Parasol

- Edible ☺
- Thick, fleshy scales on top of cap
- White spores
- White cap
- White gills
- Uniformly colored

Puffballs

- Edible ☺
- Color is white
- Rounded-shaped balls with or without spiny warts on top
- Can be mistaken for golf ball, baseball or even soccer ball

False Parasol

- Poisonous ☹
- White gills with no spores or green gills with green spores
- White to light brown stem

Slippery Jack

- Edible ☺
- Brown cap, shiny and slimy when wet
- Dark chestnut brown
- Smooth semi-matt finish in summer

Spore Print

_____
_____
_____
_____
_____
_____

Location

Site / GPS: _____ Date: _____

◯ Living Tree ◯ Leaf Litter ◯ Mulch ◯ Dead Tree or Wood ◯ Grass
◯ Soil ◯ Other _____

Type of Tree(s) On or Near: _____

Forest Type: ◯ Deciduous ◯ Coniferous ◯ Tropical ◯ Other _____

Weather Conditions: _____

General

Size (overall height): _____ Color: _____ Spore Color: _____

Texture: ◯ Tough ◯ Brittle ◯ Leathery ◯ Woody ◯ Soft ◯ Slimy
◯ Spongy ◯ Powdery ◯ Waxy ◯ Rubbery ◯ Watery (Other) _____

Bruising When Touched? ◯ Yes ◯ No Notes: _____

Structures: ◯ Cup ◯ Ring ◯ Warts _____

Cap Characteristics

Campanulate
(bell-shaped)

Conical
(triangular)

Cylindrical
(shaped like half an egg)

Convex
(outwardly rounded)

Flat
(with top of
uniform height)

Infundibuliform
(deeply, depressed,
funnel-shaped)

Depressed
(with a low
central region)

Umbonate
(with a central
bump or knob)

Surface Markings (warts, scales, slime, etc.): _____

Cap Margin: Smooth, Inrolled, Sinuous/Wavy, Other: _____

Color Changes: _____

Undercap

Gills ◯

Attachment: Free or Decurrent

Spacing: Crowded, Close,
Distant, Subdistant

Color/Bruising: _____

Pores ◯

Color: _____

Pore Size: _____

Pore Pattern: _____

Teeth ◯

Color: _____

Teeth Length: _____

Flesh: Soft or Tough

◯ Free
(gills not attached to stem)

◯ Adnexed
(gills attached narrowly to stem)

◯ Sinuate
(gills smoothly notched and running briefly down stem)

◯ Adnate
(gills widely attached widely to stem)

◯ Descending
(gills running down stem for some length)

  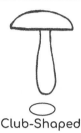  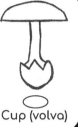

◯ Tapering

◯ Equal

◯ Club-Shaped

◯ Bulbous

◯ Cup (volva)

Chanterelle
- Edible ☺
- Shape looks like bell of a trumpet
- Bright yellow/orange
- Similar look to Jack o'Lantern

Shaggy Mane
- Edible ☺
- White shaggy cylindrical cap that turns black and inky with age
- Bell shape when mature
- Spore print is black

Morels
- Edible ☺
- Honeycombed cap
- Most morels cap is longer than stem
- Spore print is usually light colored
- Interior is hollow

Puffballs
- Edible ☺
- Color is white
- Rounded-shaped balls with or without spiny warts on top
- Can be mistaken for golf ball, baseball or even soccer ball

Meadow Mushroom
- Edible ☺
- White or whitish
- Pink gills that turn brown with age
- Closely related to portobello

False Morel
- Poisonous ☹
- Red-brown cap is irregularly lobed, like a brain
- Hollow chambers inside the cap
- Yellowish spore print

Fly Agaric
- Poisonous ☹
- Body emerges from soil looking like white eggs and turns red as it grows
- Small white to yellow pyramid-shaped warts

False Parasol
- Poisonous ☹
- White gills with no spores or green gills with green spores
- White to light brown stem

Jack O'Lantern
- Poisonous ☹
- Bright orange to yellowish
- Grows in clusters
- Cap convex
- Gills narrow
- Cream spore print

Destroying Angel
- Poisonous ☹
- White stalk and gills
- White cap or white edge and yellowish, pinkish, or tan center
- Egg-shaped cap

Shaggy Parasol
- Edible ☺
- Thick, fleshy scales on top of cap
- White spores
- White cap
- White gills
- Uniformly colored

Slippery Jack
- Edible ☺
- Brown cap, shiny and slimy when wet
- Dark chestnut brown
- Smooth semi-matt finish in summer

Spore Print

_____

_____

_____

_____

_____

_____

Location

Site / GPS: _____ Date: _____

◯ Living Tree ◯ Leaf Litter ◯ Mulch ◯ Dead Tree or Wood ◯ Grass
◯ Soil ◯ Other _____

Type of Tree(s) On or Near: _____

Forest Type: ◯ Deciduous ◯ Coniferous ◯ Tropical ◯ Other _____

Weather Conditions: _____

General

Size (overall height): _____ Color: _____ Spore Color: _____

Texture: ◯ Tough ◯ Brittle ◯ Leathery ◯ Woody ◯ Soft ◯ Slimy
◯ Spongy ◯ Powdery ◯ Waxy ◯ Rubbery ◯ Watery (Other) _____

Bruising When Touched? ◯ Yes ◯ No Notes: _____

Structures: ◯ Cup ◯ Ring ◯ Warts _____

Cap Characteristics

Campanulate
(bell-shaped)

Conical
(triangular)

Cylindrical
(shaped like half an egg)

Convex
(outwardly rounded)

Flat
(with top of
uniform height)

Infundibuliform
(deeply, depressed,
funnel-shaped)

Depressed
(with a low
central region)

Umbonate
(with a central
bump or knob)

Surface Markings (warts, scales, slime, etc.): _____

Cap Margin: Smooth, Inrolled, Sinuous/Wavy, Other: _____

Color Changes: _____

Undercap

Gills ◯
Attachment: Free or Decurrent
Spacing: Crowded, Close,
         Distant, Subdistant
Color/Bruising: _____

Pores ◯
Color: _____
Pore Size: _____
Pore Pattern: _____

Teeth ◯
Color: _____
Teeth Length: _____
Flesh: Soft or Tough

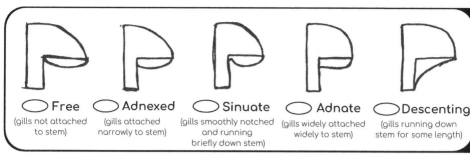

○ Free
(gills not attached to stem)

○ Adnexed
(gills attached narrowly to stem)

○ Sinuate
(gills smoothly notched and running briefly down stem)

○ Adnate
(gills widely attached widely to stem)

○ Descenting
(gills running down stem for some length)

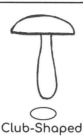
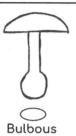
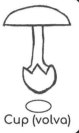

○ Tapering

○ Equal

○ Club-Shaped

○ Bulbous

○ Cup (volva)

Chanterelle

- Edible ☺
- Shape looks like bell of a trumpet
- Bright yellow/orange
- Similar look to Jack o'Lantern

Meadow Mushroom

- Edible ☺
- White or whitish
- Pink gills that turn brown with age
- Closely related to portobello

Jack O'Lantern

- Poisonous ☹
- Bright orange to yellowish
- Grows in clusters
- Cap convex
- Gills narrow
- Cream spore print

Shaggy Mane

- Edible ☺
- White shaggy cylindrical cap that turns black and inky with age
- Bell shape when mature
- Spore print is black

False Morel

- Poisonous ☹
- Red-brown cap is irregularly lobed, like a brain
- Hollow chambers inside the cap
- Yellowish spore print

Destroying Angel

- Poisonous ☹
- White stalk and gills
- White cap or white edge and yellowish, pinkish, or tan center
- Egg-shaped cap

Morels

- Edible ☺
- Honeycombed cap
- Most morels cap is longer than stem
- Spore print is usually light colored
- Interior is hollow

Fly Agaric

- Poisonous ☹
- Body emerges from soil looking like white eggs and turns red as it grows
- Small white to yellow pyramid-shaped warts

Shaggy Parasol

- Edible ☺
- Thick, fleshy scales on top of cap
- White spores
- White cap
- White gills
- Uniformly colored

Puffballs

- Edible ☺
- Color is white
- Rounded-shaped balls with or without spiny warts on top
- Can be mistaken for golf ball, baseball or even soccer ball

False Parasol

- Poisonous ☹
- White gills with no spores or green gills with green spores
- White to light brown stem

Slippery Jack

- Edible ☺
- Brown cap, shiny and slimy when wet
- Dark chestnut brown
- Smooth semi-matt finish in summer

Spore Print

Location

Site / GPS: _____ Date: _____

◯ Living Tree ◯ Leaf Litter ◯ Mulch ◯ Dead Tree or Wood ◯ Grass

◯ Soil ◯ Other _____

Type of Tree(s) On or Near: _____

Forest Type: ◯ Deciduous ◯ Coniferous ◯ Tropical ◯ Other _____

Weather Conditions: _____

General

Size (overall height): _____ Color: _____ Spore Color: _____

Texture: ◯ Tough ◯ Brittle ◯ Leathery ◯ Woody ◯ Soft ◯ Slimy

◯ Spongy ◯ Powdery ◯ Waxy ◯ Rubbery ◯ Watery (Other) _____

Bruising When Touched? ◯ Yes ◯ No Notes: _____

Structures: ◯ Cup ◯ Ring ◯ Warts _____

Cap Characteristics

Campanulate
(bell-shaped)

Conical
(triangular)

Cylindrical
(shaped like half an egg)

Convex
(outwardly rounded)

Flat
(with top of
uniform height)

Infundibuliform
(deeply, depressed,
funnel-shaped)

Depressed
(with a low
central region)

Umbonate
(with a central
bump or knob)

Surface Markings (warts, scales, slime, etc.): _____

Cap Margin: Smooth, Inrolled, Sinuous/Wavy, Other: _____

Color Changes: _____

Undercap

Gills ◯

Attachment: Free or Decurrent

Spacing: Crowded, Close,
Distant, Subdistant

Color/Bruising: _____

Pores ◯

Color: _____

Pore Size: _____

Pore Pattern: _____

Teeth ◯

Color: _____

Teeth Length: _____

Flesh: Soft or Tough

Free
(gills not attached to stem)

Adnexed
(gills attached narrowly to stem)

Sinuate
(gills smoothly notched and running briefly down stem)

Adnate
(gills widely attached widely to stem)

Descenting
(gills running down stem for some length)

  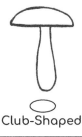 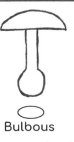 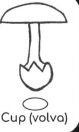

Tapering

Equal

Club-Shaped

Bulbous

Cup (volva)

Chanterelle
- Edible ☺
- Shape looks like bell of a trumpet
- Bright yellow/orange
- Similar look to Jack o'Lantern

Meadow Mushroom
- Edible ☺
- White or whitish
- Pink gills that turn brown with age
- Closely related to portobello

Jack O'Lantern
- Poisonous ☹
- Bright orange to yellowish
- Grows in clusters
- Cap convex
- Gills narrow
- Cream spore print

Shaggy Mane
- Edible ☺
- White shaggy cylindrical cap that turns black and inky with age
- Bell shape when mature
- Spore print is black

False Morel
- Poisonous ☹
- Red-brown cap is irregularly lobed, like a brain
- Hollow chambers inside the cap
- Yellowish spore print

Destroying Angel
- Poisonous ☹
- White stalk and gills
- White cap or white edge and yellowish, pinkish, or tan center
- Egg-shaped cap

Morels
- Edible ☺
- Honeycombed cap
- Most morels cap is longer than stem
- Spore print is usually light colored
- Interior is hollow

Fly Agaric
- Poisonous ☹
- Body emerges from soil looking like white eggs and turns red as it grows
- Small white to yellow pyramid-shaped warts

Shaggy Parasol
- Edible ☺
- Thick, fleshy scales on top of cap
- White spores
- White cap
- White gills
- Uniformly colored

Puffballs
- Edible ☺
- Color is white
- Rounded-shaped balls with or without spiny warts on top
- Can be mistaken for golf ball, baseball or even soccer ball

False Parasol
- Poisonous ☹
- White gills with no spores or green gills with green spores
- White to light brown stem

Slippery Jack
- Edible ☺
- Brown cap, shiny and slimy when wet
- Dark chestnut brown
- Smooth semi-matt finish in summer

Spore Print

_____
_____
_____
_____
_____
_____

Location

Site / GPS: _____ Date: _____

◯ Living Tree   ◯ Leaf Litter   ◯ Mulch   ◯ Dead Tree or Wood   ◯ Grass
◯ Soil   ◯ Other _____

Type of Tree(s) On or Near: _____

Forest Type: ◯ Deciduous   ◯ Coniferous   ◯ Tropical   ◯ Other _____

Weather Conditions: _____

General

Size (overall height): _____   Color: _____   Spore Color: _____

Texture: ◯ Tough ◯ Brittle ◯ Leathery ◯ Woody ◯ Soft ◯ Slimy
◯ Spongy   ◯ Powdery   ◯ Waxy   ◯ Rubbery   ◯ Watery   (Other) _____

Bruising When Touched?   ◯ Yes   ◯ No   Notes: _____

Structures: ◯ Cup   ◯ Ring   ◯ Warts   _____

Cap Characteristics

Campanulate
(bell-shaped)

Conical
(triangular)

Cylindrical
(shaped like half an egg)

Convex
(outwardly rounded)

Flat
(with top of
uniform height)

Infundibuliform
(deeply, depressed,
funnel-shaped)

Depressed
(with a low
central region)

Umbonate
(with a central
bump or knob)

Surface Markings (warts, scales, slime, etc.): _____

Cap Margin: Smooth, Inrolled, Sinuous/Wavy, Other: _____

Color Changes: _____

Undercap

Gills ◯

Attachment: Free or Decurrent

Spacing: Crowded, Close,
Distant, Subdistant

Color/Bruising: _____

Pores ◯

Color: _____

Pore Size: _____

Pore Pattern: _____

Teeth ◯

Color: _____

Teeth Length: _____

Flesh: Soft or Tough

○ Free
(gills not attached to stem)

○ Adnexed
(gills attached narrowly to stem)

○ Sinuate
(gills smoothly notched and running briefly down stem)

○ Adnate
(gills widely attached widely to stem)

○ Descenting
(gills running down stem for some length)

Tapering

Equal

Club-Shaped

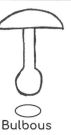

Bulbous

Cup (volva)

Chanterelle
- Edible ☺
- Shape looks like bell of a trumpet
- Bright yellow/orange
- Similar look to Jack o'Lantern

Meadow Mushroom
- Edible ☺
- White or whitish
- Pink gills that turn brown with age
- Closely related to portobello

Jack O'Lantern
- Poisonous ☹
- Bright orange to yellowish
- Grows in clusters
- Cap convex
- Gills narrow
- Cream spore print

Shaggy Mane
- Edible ☺
- White shaggy cylindrical cap that turns black and inky with age
- Bell shape when mature
- Spore print is black

False Morel
- Poisonous ☹
- Red-brown cap is irregularly lobed, like a brain
- Hollow chambers inside the cap
- Yellowish spore print

Destroying Angel
- Poisonous ☹
- White stalk and gills
- White cap or white edge and yellowish, pinkish, or tan center
- Egg-shaped cap

Morels
- Edible ☺
- Honeycombed cap
- Most morels cap is longer than stem
- Spore print is usually light colored
- Interior is hollow

Fly Agaric
- Poisonous ☹
- Body emerges from soil looking like white eggs and turns red as it grows
- Small white to yellow pyramid-shaped warts

Shaggy Parasol
- Edible ☺
- Thick, fleshy scales on top of cap
- White spores
- White cap
- White gills
- Uniformly colored

Puffballs
- Edible ☺
- Color is white
- Rounded-shaped balls with or without spiny warts on top
- Can be mistaken for golf ball, baseball or even soccer ball

False Parasol
- Poisonous ☹
- White gills with no spores or green gills with green spores
- White to light brown stem

Slippery Jack
- Edible ☺
- Brown cap, shiny and slimy when wet
- Dark chestnut brown
- Smooth semi-matt finish in summer

Spore Print

_____
_____
_____
_____
_____
_____

Location

Site / GPS: _____ Date: _____

◯ Living Tree ◯ Leaf Litter ◯ Mulch ◯ Dead Tree or Wood ◯ Grass
◯ Soil ◯ Other _____

Type of Tree(s) On or Near: _____

Forest Type: ◯ Deciduous ◯ Coniferous ◯ Tropical ◯ Other _____

Weather Conditions: _____

General

Size (overall height): _____ Color: _____ Spore Color: _____

Texture: ◯ Tough ◯ Brittle ◯ Leathery ◯ Woody ◯ Soft ◯ Slimy
◯ Spongy ◯ Powdery ◯ Waxy ◯ Rubbery ◯ Watery (Other) _____

Bruising When Touched? ◯ Yes ◯ No   Notes: _____

Structures: ◯ Cup ◯ Ring ◯ Warts   _____

Cap Characteristics

Campanulate
(bell-shaped)

Conical
(triangular)

Cylindrical
(shaped like half an egg)

Convex
(outwardly rounded)

Flat
(with top of
uniform height)

Infundibuliform
(deeply, depressed,
funnel-shaped)

Depressed
(with a low
central region)

Umbonate
(with a central
bump or knob)

Surface Markings (warts, scales, slime, etc.): _____

Cap Margin: Smooth, Inrolled, Sinuous/Wavy, Other:_____

Color Changes: _____

Undercap

Gills ◯

Attachment: Free or Decurrent

Spacing: Crowded, Close,
Distant, Subdistant

Color/Bruising: _____

Pores ◯

Color: _____

Pore Size: _____

Pore Pattern: _____

Teeth ◯

Color: _____

Teeth Length: _____

Flesh: Soft or Tough

Free
(gills not attached to stem)

Adnexed
(gills attached narrowly to stem)

Sinuate
(gills smoothly notched and running briefly down stem)

Adnate
(gills widely attached widely to stem)

Descenting
(gills running down stem for some length)

  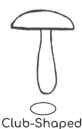 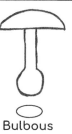 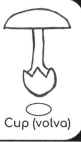

Tapering

Equal

Club-Shaped

Bulbous

Cup (volva)

Chanterelle

- Edible ☺
- Shape looks like bell of a trumpet
- Bright yellow/orange
- Similar look to Jack o'Lantern

Meadow Mushroom

- Edible ☺
- White or whitish
- Pink gills that turn brown with age
- Closely related to portobello

Jack O'Lantern

- Poisonous ☹
- Bright orange to yellowish
- Grows in clusters
- Cap convex
- Gills narrow
- Cream spore print

Shaggy Mane

- Edible ☺
- White shaggy cylindrical cap that turns black and inky with age
- Bell shape when mature
- Spore print is black

False Morel

- Poisonous ☹
- Red-brown cap is irregularly lobed, like a brain
- Hollow chambers inside the cap
- Yellowish spore print

Destroying Angel

- Poisonous ☹
- White stalk and gills
- White cap or white edge and yellowish, pinkish, or tan center
- Egg-shaped cap

Morels

- Edible ☺
- Honeycombed cap
- Most morels cap is longer than stem
- Spore print is usually light colored
- Interior is hollow

Fly Agaric

- Poisonous ☹
- Body emerges from soil looking like white eggs and turns red as it grows
- Small white to yellow pyramid-shaped warts

Shaggy Parasol

- Edible ☺
- Thick, fleshy scales on top of cap
- White spores
- White cap
- White gills
- Uniformly colored

Puffballs

- Edible ☺
- Color is white
- Rounded-shaped balls with or without spiny warts on top
- Can be mistaken for golf ball, baseball or even soccer ball

False Parasol

- Poisonous ☹
- White gills with no spores or green gills with green spores
- White to light brown stem

Slippery Jack

- Edible ☺
- Brown cap, shiny and slimy when wet
- Dark chestnut brown
- Smooth semi-matt finish in summer

Spore Print

_____
_____
_____
_____
_____
_____

Location

Site / GPS: _____ Date: _____

◯ Living Tree ◯ Leaf Litter ◯ Mulch ◯ Dead Tree or Wood ◯ Grass
◯ Soil ◯ Other _____

Type of Tree(s) On or Near: _____

Forest Type: ◯ Deciduous ◯ Coniferous ◯ Tropical ◯ Other _____

Weather Conditions: _____

General

Size (overall height): _____ Color: _____ Spore Color: _____

Texture: ◯ Tough ◯ Brittle ◯ Leathery ◯ Woody ◯ Soft ◯ Slimy
◯ Spongy ◯ Powdery ◯ Waxy ◯ Rubbery ◯ Watery (Other) _____

Bruising When Touched? ◯ Yes ◯ No Notes: _____

Structures: ◯ Cup ◯ Ring ◯ Warts _____

Cap Characteristics

Campanulate
(bell-shaped)

Conical
(triangular)

Cylindrical
(shaped like half an egg)

Convex
(outwardly rounded)

Flat
(with top of
uniform height)

Infundibuliform
(deeply, depressed,
funnel-shaped)

Depressed
(with a low
central region)

Umbonate
(with a central
bump or knob)

Surface Markings (warts, scales, slime, etc.): _____

Cap Margin: Smooth, Inrolled, Sinuous/Wavy, Other: _____

Color Changes: _____

Undercap

Gills ◯

Attachment: Free or Decurrent

Spacing: Crowded, Close,
         Distant, Subdistant

Color/Bruising: _____

Pores ◯

Color: _____

Pore Size: _____

Pore Pattern: _____

Teeth ◯

Color: _____

Teeth Length: _____

Flesh: Soft or Tough

Free	Adnexed	Sinuate	Adnate	Descenting
(gills not attached to stem)	(gills attached narrowly to stem)	(gills smoothly notched and running briefly down stem)	(gills widely attached widely to stem)	(gills running down stem for some length)

  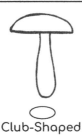  

Tapering	Equal	Club-Shaped	Bulbous	Cup (volva)

Chanterelle
- Edible ☺
- Shape looks like bell of a trumpet
- Bright yellow/orange
- Similar look to Jack o'Lantern

Meadow Mushroom
- Edible ☺
- White or whitish
- Pink gills that turn brown with age
- Closely related to portobello

Jack O'Lantern
- Poisonous ☹
- Bright orange to yellowish
- Grows in clusters
- Cap convex
- Gills narrow
- Cream spore print

Shaggy Mane
- Edible ☺
- White shaggy cylindrical cap that turns black and inky with age
- Bell shape when mature
- Spore print is black

False Morel
- Poisonous ☹
- Red-brown cap is irregularly lobed, like a brain
- Hollow chambers inside the cap
- Yellowish spore print

Destroying Angel
- Poisonous ☹
- White stalk and gills
- White cap or white edge and yellowish, pinkish, or tan center
- Egg-shaped cap

Morels
- Edible ☺
- Honeycombed cap
- Most morels cap is longer than stem
- Spore print is usually light colored
- Interior is hollow

Fly Agaric
- Poisonous ☹
- Body emerges from soil looking like white eggs and turns red as it grows
- Small white to yellow pyramid-shaped warts

Shaggy Parasol
- Edible ☺
- Thick, fleshy scales on top of cap
- White spores
- White cap
- White gills
- Uniformly colored

Puffballs
- Edible ☺
- Color is white
- Rounded-shaped balls with or without spiny warts on top
- Can be mistaken for golf ball, baseball or even soccer ball

False Parasol
- Poisonous ☹
- White gills with no spores or green gills with green spores
- White to light brown stem

Slippery Jack
- Edible ☺
- Brown cap, shiny and slimy when wet
- Dark chestnut brown
- Smooth semi-matt finish in summer

Spore Print

Location

Site / GPS: _____ Date: _____

◯ Living Tree   ◯ Leaf Litter   ◯ Mulch   ◯ Dead Tree or Wood   ◯ Grass
◯ Soil   ◯ Other _____

Type of Tree(s) On or Near: _____

Forest Type: ◯ Deciduous   ◯ Coniferous   ◯ Tropical   ◯ Other _____

Weather Conditions: _____

General

Size (overall height): _____   Color: _____   Spore Color: _____

Texture: ◯ Tough ◯ Brittle ◯ Leathery ◯ Woody ◯ Soft ◯ Slimy
◯ Spongy ◯ Powdery ◯ Waxy ◯ Rubbery ◯ Watery (Other) _____

Bruising When Touched? ◯ Yes ◯ No   Notes: _____

Structures: ◯ Cup ◯ Ring ◯ Warts   _____

Cap Characteristics

Campanulate
(bell-shaped)

Conical
(triangular)

Cylindrical
(shaped like half an egg)

Convex
(outwardly rounded)

Flat
(with top of uniform height)

Infundibuliform
(deeply, depressed, funnel-shaped)

Depressed
(with a low central region)

Umbonate
(with a central bump or knob)

Surface Markings (warts, scales, slime, etc.): _____

Cap Margin: Smooth, Inrolled, Sinuous/Wavy, Other: _____

Color Changes: _____

Undercap

Gills ◯
Attachment: Free or Decurrent
Spacing: Crowded, Close,
         Distant, Subdistant
Color/Bruising: _____

Pores ◯
Color: _____
Pore Size: _____
Pore Pattern: _____

Teeth ◯
Color: _____
Teeth Length: _____
Flesh: Soft or Tough

⬭ Free
(gills not attached to stem)

⬭ Adnexed
(gills attached narrowly to stem)

⬭ Sinuate
(gills smoothly notched and running briefly down stem)

⬭ Adnate
(gills widely attached widely to stem)

⬭ Descenting
(gills running down stem for some length)

  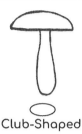 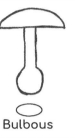 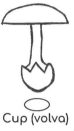

⬭ Tapering

⬭ Equal

⬭ Club-Shaped

⬭ Bulbous

⬭ Cup (volva)

Chanterelle
- Edible ☺
- Shape looks like bell of a trumpet
- Bright yellow/orange
- Similar look to Jack o'Lantern

Meadow Mushroom
- Edible ☺
- White or whitish
- Pink gills that turn brown with age
- Closely related to portobello

Jack O'Lantern
- Poisonous ☹
- Bright orange to yellowish
- Grows in clusters
- Cap convex
- Gills narrow
- Cream spore print

Shaggy Mane
- Edible ☺
- White shaggy cylindrical cap that turns black and inky with age
- Bell shape when mature
- Spore print is black

False Morel
- Poisonous ☹
- Red-brown cap is irregularly lobed, like a brain
- Hollow chambers inside the cap
- Yellowish spore print

Destroying Angel
- Poisonous ☹
- White stalk and gills
- White cap or white edge and yellowish, pinkish, or tan center
- Egg-shaped cap

Morels
- Edible ☺
- Honeycombed cap
- Most morels cap is longer than stem
- Spore print is usually light colored
- Interior is hollow

Fly Agaric
- Poisonous ☹
- Body emerges from soil looking like white eggs and turns red as it grows
- Small white to yellow pyramid-shaped warts

Shaggy Parasol
- Edible ☺
- Thick, fleshy scales on top of cap
- White spores
- White cap
- White gills
- Uniformly colored

Puffballs
- Edible ☺
- Color is white
- Rounded-shaped balls with or without spiny warts on top
- Can be mistaken for golf ball, baseball or even soccer ball

False Parasol
- Poisonous ☹
- White gills with no spores or green gills with green spores
- White to light brown stem

Slippery Jack
- Edible ☺
- Brown cap, shiny and slimy when wet
- Dark chestnut brown
- Smooth semi-matt finish in summer

Spore Print

_____
_____
_____
_____
_____
_____

Location

Site / GPS: _____ Date: _____

○ Living Tree ○ Leaf Litter ○ Mulch ○ Dead Tree or Wood ○ Grass
○ Soil ○ Other _____

Type of Tree(s) On or Near: _____

Forest Type: ○ Deciduous ○ Coniferous ○ Tropical ○ Other _____

Weather Conditions: _____

General

Size (overall height): _____ Color: _____ Spore Color: _____

Texture: ○ Tough ○ Brittle ○ Leathery ○ Woody ○ Soft ○ Slimy
○ Spongy ○ Powdery ○ Waxy ○ Rubbery ○ Watery (Other) _____

Bruising When Touched? ○ Yes ○ No   Notes: _____

Structures: ○ Cup ○ Ring ○ Warts   _____

Cap Characteristics

Campanulate
(bell-shaped)

Conical
(triangular)

Cylindrical
(shaped like half an egg)

Convex
(outwardly rounded)

Flat
(with top of uniform height)

Infundibuliform
(deeply, depressed, funnel-shaped)

Depressed
(with a low central region)

Umbonate
(with a central bump or knob)

Surface Markings (warts, scales, slime, etc.): _____

Cap Margin: Smooth, Inrolled, Sinuous/Wavy, Other: _____

Color Changes: _____

Undercap

Gills ○

Attachment: Free or Decurrent

Spacing: Crowded, Close, Distant, Subdistant

Color/Bruising: _____

Pores ○

Color: _____

Pore Size: _____

Pore Pattern: _____

Teeth ○

Color: _____

Teeth Length: _____

Flesh: Soft or Tough

○ Free
(gills not attached to stem)

○ Adnexed
(gills attached narrowly to stem)

○ Sinuate
(gills smoothly notched and running briefly down stem)

○ Adnate
(gills widely attached widely to stem)

○ Descenting
(gills running down stem for some length)

Tapering

Equal

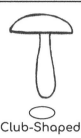

Club-Shaped

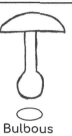

Bulbous

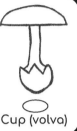

Cup (volva)

Chanterelle
- Edible ☺
- Shape looks like bell of a trumpet
- Bright yellow/orange
- Similar look to Jack o'Lantern

Meadow Mushroom
- Edible ☺
- White or whitish
- Pink gills that turn brown with age
- Closely related to portobello

Jack O'Lantern
- Poisonous ☹
- Bright orange to yellowish
- Grows in clusters
- Cap convex
- Gills narrow
- Cream spore print

Shaggy Mane
- Edible ☺
- White shaggy cylindrical cap that turns black and inky with age
- Bell shape when mature
- Spore print is black

False Morel
- Poisonous ☹
- Red-brown cap is irregularly lobed, like a brain
- Hollow chambers inside the cap
- Yellowish spore print

Destroying Angel
- Poisonous ☹
- White stalk and gills
- White cap or white edge and yellowish, pinkish, or tan center
- Egg-shaped cap

Morels
- Edible ☺
- Honeycombed cap
- Most morels cap is longer than stem
- Spore print is usually light colored
- Interior is hollow

Fly Agaric
- Poisonous ☹
- Body emerges from soil looking like white eggs and turns red as it grows
- Small white to yellow pyramid-shaped warts

Shaggy Parasol
- Edible ☺
- Thick, fleshy scales on top of cap
- White spores
- White cap
- White gills
- Uniformly colored

Puffballs
- Edible ☺
- Color is white
- Rounded-shaped balls with or without spiny warts on top
- Can be mistaken for golf ball, baseball or even soccer ball

False Parasol
- Poisonous ☹
- White gills with no spores or green gills with green spores
- White to light brown stem

Slippery Jack
- Edible ☺
- Brown cap, shiny and slimy when wet
- Dark chestnut brown
- Smooth semi-matt finish in summer

Spore Print

Location

Site / GPS: _____ Date: _____

○ Living Tree ○ Leaf Litter ○ Mulch ○ Dead Tree or Wood ○ Grass
○ Soil ○ Other _____

Type of Tree(s) On or Near: _____

Forest Type: ○ Deciduous ○ Coniferous ○ Tropical ○ Other _____

Weather Conditions: _____

General

Size (overall height): _____ Color: _____ Spore Color: _____

Texture: ○ Tough ○ Brittle ○ Leathery ○ Woody ○ Soft ○ Slimy
○ Spongy ○ Powdery ○ Waxy ○ Rubbery ○ Watery (Other) _____

Bruising When Touched? ○ Yes ○ No   Notes: _____

Structures: ○ Cup ○ Ring ○ Warts   _____

Cap Characteristics

Campanulate
(bell-shaped)

Conical
(triangular)

Cylindrical
(shaped like half an egg)

Convex
(outwardly rounded)

Flat
(with top of
uniform height)

Infundibuliform
(deeply, depressed,
funnel-shaped)

Depressed
(with a low
central region)

Umbonate
(with a central
bump or knob)

Surface Markings (warts, scales, slime, etc.): _____

Cap Margin: Smooth, Inrolled, Sinuous/Wavy, Other: _____

Color Changes: _____

Undercap

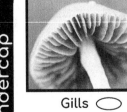

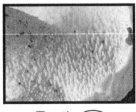

Gills ○

Attachment: Free or Decurrent

Spacing: Crowded, Close,
Distant, Subdistant

Color/Bruising: _____

Pores ○

Color: _____

Pore Size: _____

Pore Pattern: _____

Teeth ○

Color: _____

Teeth Length: _____

Flesh: Soft or Tough

○ Free
(gills not attached to stem)

○ Adnexed
(gills attached narrowly to stem)

○ Sinuate
(gills smoothly notched and running briefly down stem)

○ Adnate
(gills widely attached widely to stem)

○ Descenting
(gills running down stem for some length)

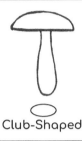

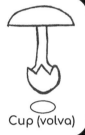

○ Tapering

○ Equal

Club-Shaped

Bulbous

Cup (volva)

Chanterelle

- Edible ☺
- Shape looks like bell of a trumpet
- Bright yellow/orange
- Similar look to Jack o'Lantern

Meadow Mushroom

- Edible ☺
- White or whitish
- Pink gills that turn brown with age
- Closely related to portobello

Jack O'Lantern

- Poisonous ☹
- Bright orange to yellowish
- Grows in clusters
- Cap convex
- Gills narrow
- Cream spore print

Shaggy Mane

- Edible ☺
- White shaggy cylindrical cap that turns black and inky with age
- Bell shape when mature
- Spore print is black

False Morel

- Poisonous ☹
- Red-brown cap is irregularly lobed, like a brain
- Hollow chambers inside the cap
- Yellowish spore print

Destroying Angel

- Poisonous ☹
- White stalk and gills
- White cap or white edge and yellowish, pinkish, or tan center
- Egg-shaped cap

Morels

- Edible ☺
- Honeycombed cap
- Most morels cap is longer than stem
- Spore print is usually light colored
- Interior is hollow

Fly Agaric

- Poisonous ☹
- Body emerges from soil looking like white eggs and turns red as it grows
- Small white to yellow pyramid-shaped warts

Shaggy Parasol

- Edible ☺
- Thick, fleshy scales on top of cap
- White spores
- White cap
- White gills
- Uniformly colored

Puffballs

- Edible ☺
- Color is white
- Rounded-shaped balls with or without spiny warts on top
- Can be mistaken for golf ball, baseball or even soccer ball

False Parasol

- Poisonous ☹
- White gills with no spores or green gills with green spores
- White to light brown stem

Slippery Jack

- Edible ☺
- Brown cap, shiny and slimy when wet
- Dark chestnut brown
- Smooth semi-matt finish in summer

Spore Print

_____
_____
_____
_____
_____
_____

Location

Site / GPS: _____ Date: _____

◯ Living Tree ◯ Leaf Litter ◯ Mulch ◯ Dead Tree or Wood ◯ Grass
◯ Soil ◯ Other _____

Type of Tree(s) On or Near: _____

Forest Type: ◯ Deciduous ◯ Coniferous ◯ Tropical ◯ Other _____

Weather Conditions: _____

General

Size (overall height): _____ Color: _____ Spore Color: _____

Texture: ◯ Tough ◯ Brittle ◯ Leathery ◯ Woody ◯ Soft ◯ Slimy
◯ Spongy ◯ Powdery ◯ Waxy ◯ Rubbery ◯ Watery (Other) _____

Bruising When Touched? ◯ Yes ◯ No Notes: _____

Structures: ◯ Cup ◯ Ring ◯ Warts   _____

Cap Characteristics

Campanulate
(bell-shaped)

Conical
(triangular)

Cylindrical
(shaped like half an egg)

Convex
(outwardly rounded)

Flat
(with top of
uniform height)

Infundibuliform
(deeply, depressed,
funnel-shaped)

Depressed
(with a low
central region)

Umbonate
(with a central
bump or knob)

Surface Markings (warts, scales, slime, etc.): _____

Cap Margin: Smooth, Inrolled, Sinuous/Wavy, Other: _____

Color Changes: _____

Undercap

Gills ◯

Attachment: Free or Decurrent

Spacing: Crowded, Close,
Distant, Subdistant

Color/Bruising: _____

Pores ◯

Color: _____

Pore Size: _____

Pore Pattern: _____

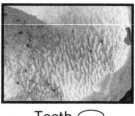

Teeth ◯

Color: _____

Teeth Length: _____

Flesh: Soft or Tough

Free
(gills not attached to stem)

Adnexed
(gills attached narrowly to stem)

Sinuate
(gills smoothly notched and running briefly down stem)

Adnate
(gills widely attached widely to stem)

Descending
(gills running down stem for some length)

Tapering

Equal

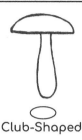

Club-Shaped

Bulbous

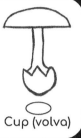

Cup (volva)

Chanterelle

- Edible ☺
- Shape looks like bell of a trumpet
- Bright yellow/orange
- Similar look to Jack o'Lantern

Meadow Mushroom

- Edible ☺
- White or whitish
- Pink gills that turn brown with age
- Closely related to portobello

Jack O'Lantern

- Poisonous ☹
- Bright orange to yellowish
- Grows in clusters
- Cap convex
- Gills narrow
- Cream spore print

Shaggy Mane

- Edible ☺
- White shaggy cylindrical cap that turns black and inky with age
- Bell shape when mature
- Spore print is black

False Morel

- Poisonous ☹
- Red-brown cap is irregularly lobed, like a brain
- Hollow chambers inside the cap
- Yellowish spore print

Destroying Angel

- Poisonous ☹
- White stalk and gills
- White cap or white edge and yellowish, pinkish, or tan center
- Egg-shaped cap

Morels

- Edible ☺
- Honeycombed cap
- Most morels cap is longer than stem
- Spore print is usually light colored
- Interior is hollow

Fly Agaric

- Poisonous ☹
- Body emerges from soil looking like white eggs and turns red as it grows
- Small white to yellow pyramid-shaped warts

Shaggy Parasol

- Edible ☺
- Thick, fleshy scales on top of cap
- White spores
- White cap
- White gills
- Uniformly colored

Puffballs

- Edible ☺
- Color is white
- Rounded-shaped balls with or without spiny warts on top
- Can be mistaken for golf ball, baseball or even soccer ball

False Parasol

- Poisonous ☹
- White gills with no spores or green gills with green spores
- White to light brown stem

Slippery Jack

- Edible ☺
- Brown cap, shiny and slimy when wet
- Dark chestnut brown
- Smooth semi-matt finish in summer

Spore Print

Location

Site / GPS: _____ Date: _____

○ Living Tree ○ Leaf Litter ○ Mulch ○ Dead Tree or Wood ○ Grass
○ Soil ○ Other _____

Type of Tree(s) On or Near: _____

Forest Type: ○ Deciduous ○ Coniferous ○ Tropical ○ Other _____

Weather Conditions: _____

General

Size (overall height): _____ Color: _____ Spore Color: _____

Texture: ○ Tough ○ Brittle ○ Leathery ○ Woody ○ Soft ○ Slimy
○ Spongy ○ Powdery ○ Waxy ○ Rubbery ○ Watery (Other) _____

Bruising When Touched? ○ Yes ○ No Notes: _____

Structures: ○ Cup ○ Ring ○ Warts _____

Cap Characteristics

Campanulate
(bell-shaped)

Conical
(triangular)

Cylindrical
(shaped like half an egg)

Convex
(outwardly rounded)

Flat
(with top of uniform height)

Infundibuliform
(deeply, depressed, funnel-shaped)

Depressed
(with a low central region)

Umbonate
(with a central bump or knob)

Surface Markings (warts, scales, slime, etc.): _____

Cap Margin: Smooth, Inrolled, Sinuous/Wavy, Other: _____

Color Changes: _____

Undercap

Gills ○
Attachment: Free or Decurrent
Spacing: Crowded, Close, Distant, Subdistant
Color/Bruising: _____

Pores ○
Color: _____
Pore Size: _____
Pore Pattern: _____

Teeth ○
Color: _____
Teeth Length: _____
Flesh: Soft or Tough

○ Free
(gills not attached to stem)

○ Adnexed
(gills attached narrowly to stem)

○ Sinuate
(gills smoothly notched and running briefly down stem)

○ Adnate
(gills widely attached widely to stem)

○ Descenting
(gills running down stem for some length)

  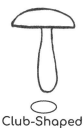 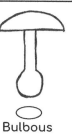 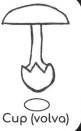

○ Tapering

○ Equal

○ Club-Shaped

○ Bulbous

○ Cup (volva)

Chanterelle
- Edible ☺
- Shape looks like bell of a trumpet
- Bright yellow/orange
- Similar look to Jack o'Lantern

Meadow Mushroom
- Edible ☺
- White or whitish
- Pink gills that turn brown with age
- Closely related to portobello

Jack O'Lantern
- Poisonous ☹
- Bright orange to yellowish
- Grows in clusters
- Cap convex
- Gills narrow
- Cream spore print

Shaggy Mane
- Edible ☺
- White shaggy cylindrical cap that turns black and inky with age
- Bell shape when mature
- Spore print is black

False Morel
- Poisonous ☹
- Red-brown cap is irregularly lobed, like a brain
- Hollow chambers inside the cap
- Yellowish spore print

Destroying Angel
- Poisonous ☹
- White stalk and gills
- White cap or white edge and yellowish, pinkish, or tan center
- Egg-shaped cap

Morels
- Edible ☺
- Honeycombed cap
- Most morels cap is longer than stem
- Spore print is usually light colored
- Interior is hollow

Fly Agaric
- Poisonous ☹
- Body emerges from soil looking like white eggs and turns red as it grows
- Small white to yellow pyramid-shaped warts

Shaggy Parasol
- Edible ☺
- Thick, fleshy scales on top of cap
- White spores
- White cap
- White gills
- Uniformly colored

Puffballs
- Edible ☺
- Color is white
- Rounded-shaped balls with or without spiny warts on top
- Can be mistaken for golf ball, baseball or even soccer ball

False Parasol
- Poisonous ☹
- White gills with no spores or green gills with green spores
- White to light brown stem

Slippery Jack
- Edible ☺
- Brown cap, shiny and slimy when wet
- Dark chestnut brown
- Smooth semi-matt finish in summer

Spore Print

_____
_____
_____
_____
_____
_____

Location

Site / GPS: _____ Date: _____

○ Living Tree   ○ Leaf Litter   ○ Mulch   ○ Dead Tree or Wood   ○ Grass
○ Soil   ○ Other _____

Type of Tree(s) On or Near: _____

Forest Type: ○ Deciduous   ○ Coniferous   ○ Tropical   ○ Other _____

Weather Conditions: _____

General

Size (overall height): _____   Color: _____   Spore Color: _____

Texture: ○ Tough ○ Brittle ○ Leathery ○ Woody ○ Soft ○ Slimy
○ Spongy   ○ Powdery   ○ Waxy   ○ Rubbery   ○ Watery   (Other) _____

Bruising When Touched? ○ Yes ○ No   Notes: _____

Structures: ○ Cup ○ Ring ○ Warts   _____

Cap Characteristics

Campanulate
(bell-shaped)

Conical
(triangular)

Cylindrical
(shaped like half an egg)

Convex
(outwardly rounded)

Flat
(with top of
uniform height)

Infundibuliform
(deeply, depressed,
funnel-shaped)

Depressed
(with a low
central region)

Umbonate
(with a central
bump or knob)

Surface Markings (warts, scales, slime, etc.): _____

Cap Margin: Smooth, Inrolled, Sinuous/Wavy, Other: _____

Color Changes: _____

Undercap

Gills ○

Attachment: Free or Decurrent

Spacing: Crowded, Close,
Distant, Subdistant

Color/Bruising: _____

Pores ○

Color: _____

Pore Size: _____

Pore Pattern: _____

Teeth ○

Color: _____

Teeth Length: _____

Flesh: Soft or Tough

○ Free
(gills not attached to stem)

○ Adnexed
(gills attached narrowly to stem)

○ Sinuate
(gills smoothly notched and running briefly down stem)

○ Adnate
(gills widely attached widely to stem)

○ Descending
(gills running down stem for some length)

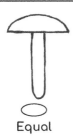

○ Tapering

○ Equal

○ Club-Shaped

○ Bulbous

○ Cup (volva)

Chanterelle

- Edible ☺
- Shape looks like bell of a trumpet
- Bright yellow/orange
- Similar look to Jack o'Lantern

Meadow Mushroom

- Edible ☺
- White or whitish
- Pink gills that turn brown with age
- Closely related to portobello

Jack O'Lantern

- Poisonous ☹
- Bright orange to yellowish
- Grows in clusters
- Cap convex
- Gills narrow
- Cream spore print

Shaggy Mane

- Edible ☺
- White shaggy cylindrical cap that turns black and inky with age
- Bell shape when mature
- Spore print is black

False Morel

- Poisonous ☹
- Red-brown cap is irregularly lobed, like a brain
- Hollow chambers inside the cap
- Yellowish spore print

Destroying Angel

- Poisonous ☹
- White stalk and gills
- White cap or white edge and yellowish, pinkish, or tan center
- Egg-shaped cap

Morels

- Edible ☺
- Honeycombed cap
- Most morels cap is longer than stem
- Spore print is usually light colored
- Interior is hollow

Fly Agaric

- Poisonous ☹
- Body emerges from soil looking like white eggs and turns red as it grows
- Small white to yellow pyramid-shaped warts

Shaggy Parasol

- Edible ☺
- Thick, fleshy scales on top of cap
- White spores
- White cap
- White gills
- Uniformly colored

Puffballs

- Edible ☺
- Color is white
- Rounded-shaped balls with or without spiny warts on top
- Can be mistaken for golf ball, baseball or even soccer ball

False Parasol

- Poisonous ☹
- White gills with no spores or green gills with green spores
- White to light brown stem

Slippery Jack

- Edible ☺
- Brown cap, shiny and slimy when wet
- Dark chestnut brown
- Smooth semi-matt finish in summer

Spore Print

_____
_____
_____
_____
_____
_____

Location

Site / GPS: _____ Date: _____

◯ Living Tree ◯ Leaf Litter ◯ Mulch ◯ Dead Tree or Wood ◯ Grass
◯ Soil ◯ Other _____

Type of Tree(s) On or Near: _____

Forest Type: ◯ Deciduous ◯ Coniferous ◯ Tropical ◯ Other _____

Weather Conditions: _____

General

Size (overall height): _____ Color: _____ Spore Color: _____

Texture: ◯ Tough ◯ Brittle ◯ Leathery ◯ Woody ◯ Soft ◯ Slimy
◯ Spongy ◯ Powdery ◯ Waxy ◯ Rubbery ◯ Watery (Other) _____

Bruising When Touched? ◯ Yes ◯ No   Notes: _____

Structures: ◯ Cup ◯ Ring ◯ Warts   _____

Cap Characteristics

Campanulate
(bell-shaped)

Conical
(triangular)

Cylindrical
(shaped like half an egg)

Convex
(outwardly rounded)

Flat
(with top of
uniform height)

Infundibuliform
(deeply, depressed,
funnel-shaped)

Depressed
(with a low
central region)

Umbonate
(with a central
bump or knob)

Surface Markings (warts, scales, slime, etc.): _____

Cap Margin: Smooth, Inrolled, Sinuous/Wavy, Other: _____

Color Changes: _____

Undercap

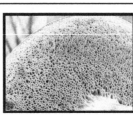

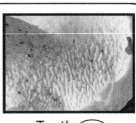

Gills ◯

Attachment: Free or Decurrent

Spacing: Crowded, Close,
Distant, Subdistant

Color/Bruising: _____

Pores ◯

Color: _____

Pore Size: _____

Pore Pattern: _____

Teeth ◯

Color: _____

Teeth Length: _____

Flesh: Soft or Tough

Free	Adnexed	Sinuate	Adnate	Descenting
(gills not attached to stem)	(gills attached narrowly to stem)	(gills smoothly notched and running briefly down stem)	(gills widely attached widely to stem)	(gills running down stem for some length)

   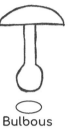 

Tapering	Equal	Club-Shaped	Bulbous	Cup (volva)

Chanterelle
- Edible ☺
- Shape looks like bell of a trumpet
- Bright yellow/orange
- Similar look to Jack o'Lantern

Meadow Mushroom
- Edible ☺
- White or whitish
- Pink gills that turn brown with age
- Closely related to portobello

Jack O'Lantern
- Poisonous ☹
- Bright orange to yellowish
- Grows in clusters
- Cap convex
- Gills narrow
- Cream spore print

Shaggy Mane
- Edible ☺
- White shaggy cylindrical cap that turns black and inky with age
- Bell shape when mature
- Spore print is black

False Morel
- Poisonous ☹
- Red-brown cap is irregularly lobed, like a brain
- Hollow chambers inside the cap
- Yellowish spore print

Destroying Angel
- Poisonous ☹
- White stalk and gills
- White cap or white edge and yellowish, pinkish, or tan center
- Egg-shaped cap

Morels
- Edible ☺
- Honeycombed cap
- Most morels cap is longer than stem
- Spore print is usually light colored
- Interior is hollow

Fly Agaric
- Poisonous ☹
- Body emerges from soil looking like white eggs and turns red as it grows
- Small white to yellow pyramid-shaped warts

Shaggy Parasol
- Edible ☺
- Thick, fleshy scales on top of cap
- White spores
- White cap
- White gills
- Uniformly colored

Puffballs
- Edible ☺
- Color is white
- Rounded-shaped balls with or without spiny warts on top
- Can be mistaken for golf ball, baseball or even soccer ball

False Parasol
- Poisonous ☹
- White gills with no spores or green gills with green spores
- White to light brown stem

Slippery Jack
- Edible ☺
- Brown cap, shiny and slimy when wet
- Dark chestnut brown
- Smooth semi-matt finish in summer

Spore Print

Location

Site / GPS: _____ Date: _____

◯ Living Tree ◯ Leaf Litter ◯ Mulch ◯ Dead Tree or Wood ◯ Grass
◯ Soil ◯ Other _____

Type of Tree(s) On or Near: _____

Forest Type: ◯ Deciduous ◯ Coniferous ◯ Tropical ◯ Other _____

Weather Conditions: _____

General

Size (overall height): _____ Color: _____ Spore Color: _____

Texture: ◯ Tough ◯ Brittle ◯ Leathery ◯ Woody ◯ Soft ◯ Slimy
◯ Spongy ◯ Powdery ◯ Waxy ◯ Rubbery ◯ Watery (Other) _____

Bruising When Touched? ◯ Yes ◯ No   Notes: _____

Structures: ◯ Cup ◯ Ring ◯ Warts   _____

Cap Characteristics

Campanulate
(bell-shaped)

Conical
(triangular)

Cylindrical
(shaped like half an egg)

Convex
(outwardly rounded)

Flat
(with top of
uniform height)

Infundibuliform
(deeply, depressed,
funnel-shaped)

Depressed
(with a low
central region)

Umbonate
(with a central
bump or knob)

Surface Markings (warts, scales, slime, etc.): _____

Cap Margin: Smooth, Inrolled, Sinuous/Wavy, Other:_____

Color Changes: _____

Undercap

Gills ◯

Attachment: Free or Decurrent

Spacing: Crowded, Close,
Distant, Subdistant

Color/Bruising: _____

Pores ◯

Color: _____

Pore Size: _____

Pore Pattern: _____

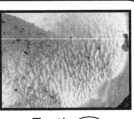

Teeth ◯

Color: _____

Teeth Length: _____

Flesh: Soft or Tough

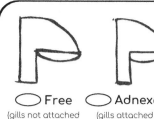

○ Free
(gills not attached to stem)

○ Adnexed
(gills attached narrowly to stem)

○ Sinuate
(gills smoothly notched and running briefly down stem)

○ Adnate
(gills widely attached widely to stem)

○ Descenting
(gills running down stem for some length)

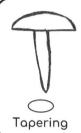

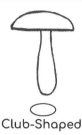

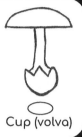

Tapering

Equal

Club-Shaped

Bulbous

Cup (volva)

Chanterelle
- Edible ☺
- Shape looks like bell of a trumpet
- Bright yellow/orange
- Similar look to Jack o'Lantern

Meadow Mushroom
- Edible ☺
- White or whitish
- Pink gills that turn brown with age
- Closely related to portobello

Jack O'Lantern
- Poisonous ☹
- Bright orange to yellowish
- Grows in clusters
- Cap convex
- Gills narrow
- Cream spore print

Shaggy Mane
- Edible ☺
- White shaggy cylindrical cap that turns black and inky with age
- Bell shape when mature
- Spore print is black

False Morel
- Poisonous ☹
- Red-brown cap is irregularly lobed, like a brain
- Hollow chambers inside the cap
- Yellowish spore print

Destroying Angel
- Poisonous ☹
- White stalk and gills
- White cap or white edge and yellowish, pinkish, or tan center
- Egg-shaped cap

Morels
- Edible ☺
- Honeycombed cap
- Most morels cap is longer than stem
- Spore print is usually light colored
- Interior is hollow

Fly Agaric
- Poisonous ☹
- Body emerges from soil looking like white eggs and turns red as it grows
- Small white to yellow pyramid-shaped warts

Shaggy Parasol
- Edible ☺
- Thick, fleshy scales on top of cap
- White spores
- White cap
- White gills
- Uniformly colored

Puffballs
- Edible ☺
- Color is white
- Rounded-shaped balls with or without spiny warts on top
- Can be mistaken for golf ball, baseball or even soccer ball

False Parasol
- Poisonous ☹
- White gills with no spores or green gills with green spores
- White to light brown stem

Slippery Jack
- Edible ☺
- Brown cap, shiny and slimy when wet
- Dark chestnut brown
- Smooth semi-matt finish in summer

Spore Print

_____
_____
_____
_____
_____
_____

Location

Site / GPS: _____ Date: _____

○ Living Tree ○ Leaf Litter ○ Mulch ○ Dead Tree or Wood ○ Grass
○ Soil ○ Other _____

Type of Tree(s) On or Near: _____

Forest Type: ○ Deciduous ○ Coniferous ○ Tropical ○ Other _____

Weather Conditions: _____

General

Size (overall height): _____ Color: _____ Spore Color: _____

Texture: ○ Tough ○ Brittle ○ Leathery ○ Woody ○ Soft ○ Slimy
○ Spongy ○ Powdery ○ Waxy ○ Rubbery ○ Watery (Other) _____

Bruising When Touched? ○ Yes ○ No   Notes: _____

Structures: ○ Cup ○ Ring ○ Warts   _____

Cap Characteristics

Campanulate
(bell-shaped)

Conical
(triangular)

Cylindrical
(shaped like half an egg)

Convex
(outwardly rounded)

Flat
(with top of
uniform height)

Infundibuliform
(deeply, depressed,
funnel-shaped)

Depressed
(with a low
central region)

Umbonate
(with a central
bump or knob)

Surface Markings (warts, scales, slime, etc.): _____

Cap Margin: Smooth, Inrolled, Sinuous/Wavy, Other: _____

Color Changes: _____

Undercap

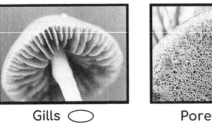

Gills ○

Attachment: Free or Decurrent

Spacing: Crowded, Close,
Distant, Subdistant

Color/Bruising: _____

Pores ○

Color: _____

Pore Size: _____

Pore Pattern: _____

Teeth ○

Color: _____

Teeth Length: _____

Flesh: Soft or Tough

○ **Free**
(gills not attached to stem)

○ **Adnexed**
(gills attached narrowly to stem)

○ **Sinuate**
(gills smoothly notched and running briefly down stem)

○ **Adnate**
(gills widely attached widely to stem)

○ **Descenting**
(gills running down stem for some length)

    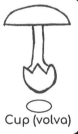

○ **Tapering** ○ **Equal** ○ **Club-Shaped** ○ **Bulbous** ○ **Cup (volva)**

Chanterelle

- Edible ☺
- Shape looks like bell of a trumpet
- Bright yellow/orange
- Similar look to Jack o'Lantern

Meadow Mushroom

- Edible ☺
- White or whitish
- Pink gills that turn brown with age
- Closely related to portobello

Jack O'Lantern

- Poisonous ☹
- Bright orange to yellowish
- Grows in clusters
- Cap convex
- Gills narrow
- Cream spore print

Shaggy Mane

- Edible ☺
- White shaggy cylindrical cap that turns black and inky with age
- Bell shape when mature
- Spore print is black

False Morel

- Poisonous ☹
- Red-brown cap is irregularly lobed, like a brain
- Hollow chambers inside the cap
- Yellowish spore print

Destroying Angel

- Poisonous ☹
- White stalk and gills
- White cap or white edge and yellowish, pinkish, or tan center
- Egg-shaped cap

Morels

- Edible ☺
- Honeycombed cap
- Most morels cap is longer than stem
- Spore print is usually light colored
- Interior is hollow

Fly Agaric

- Poisonous ☹
- Body emerges from soil looking like white eggs and turns red as it grows
- Small white to yellow pyramid-shaped warts

Shaggy Parasol

- Edible ☺
- Thick, fleshy scales on top of cap
- White spores
- White cap
- White gills
- Uniformly colored

Puffballs

- Edible ☺
- Color is white
- Rounded-shaped balls with or without spiny warts on top
- Can be mistaken for golf ball, baseball or even soccer ball

False Parasol

- Poisonous ☹
- White gills with no spores or green gills with green spores
- White to light brown stem

Slippery Jack

- Edible ☺
- Brown cap, shiny and slimy when wet
- Dark chestnut brown
- Smooth semi-matt finish in summer

Spore Print

_____

_____

_____

_____

_____

_____

Location

Site / GPS: _____ Date: _____

○ Living Tree ○ Leaf Litter ○ Mulch ○ Dead Tree or Wood ○ Grass
○ Soil ○ Other _____

Type of Tree(s) On or Near: _____

Forest Type: ○ Deciduous ○ Coniferous ○ Tropical ○ Other _____

Weather Conditions: _____

General

Size (overall height): _____ Color: _____ Spore Color: _____

Texture: ○ Tough ○ Brittle ○ Leathery ○ Woody ○ Soft ○ Slimy
○ Spongy ○ Powdery ○ Waxy ○ Rubbery ○ Watery (Other) _____

Bruising When Touched? ○ Yes ○ No   Notes: _____

Structures: ○ Cup ○ Ring ○ Warts   _____

Cap Characteristics

Campanulate
(bell-shaped)

Conical
(triangular)

Cylindrical
(shaped like half an egg)

Convex
(outwardly rounded)

Flat
(with top of uniform height)

Infundibuliform
(deeply, depressed, funnel-shaped)

Depressed
(with a low central region)

Umbonate
(with a central bump or knob)

Surface Markings (warts, scales, slime, etc.): _____

Cap Margin: Smooth, Inrolled, Sinuous/Wavy, Other:_____

Color Changes: _____

Undercap

Gills ○
Attachment: Free or Decurrent
Spacing: Crowded, Close,
        Distant, Subdistant
Color/Bruising: _____

Pores ○
Color: _____
Pore Size: _____
Pore Pattern: _____

Teeth ○
Color: _____
Teeth Length: _____
Flesh: Soft or Tough

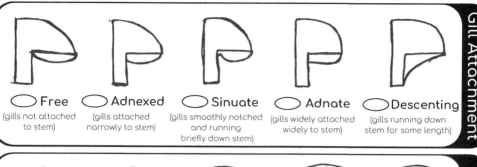

○ Free
(gills not attached to stem)

○ Adnexed
(gills attached narrowly to stem)

○ Sinuate
(gills smoothly notched and running briefly down stem)

○ Adnate
(gills widely attached widely to stem)

○ Descenting
(gills running down stem for some length)

    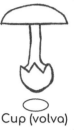

Tapering   **Equal**   **Club-Shaped**   **Bulbous**   **Cup (volva)**

Chanterelle
- Edible ☺
- Shape looks like bell of a trumpet
- Bright yellow/orange
- Similar look to Jack o'Lantern

Meadow Mushroom
- Edible ☺
- White or whitish
- Pink gills that turn brown with age
- Closely related to portobello

Jack O'Lantern
- Poisonous ☹
- Bright orange to yellowish
- Grows in clusters
- Cap convex
- Gills narrow
- Cream spore print

Shaggy Mane
- Edible ☺
- White shaggy cylindrical cap that turns black and inky with age
- Bell shape when mature
- Spore print is black

False Morel
- Poisonous ☹
- Red-brown cap is irregularly lobed, like a brain
- Hollow chambers inside the cap
- Yellowish spore print

Destroying Angel
- Poisonous ☹
- White stalk and gills
- White cap or white edge and yellowish, pinkish, or tan center
- Egg-shaped cap

Morels
- Edible ☺
- Honeycombed cap
- Most morels cap is longer than stem
- Spore print is usually light colored
- Interior is hollow

Fly Agaric
- Poisonous ☹
- Body emerges from soil looking like white eggs and turns red as it grows
- Small white to yellow pyramid-shaped warts

Shaggy Parasol
- Edible ☺
- Thick, fleshy scales on top of cap
- White spores
- White cap
- White gills
- Uniformly colored

Puffballs
- Edible ☺
- Color is white
- Rounded-shaped balls with or without spiny warts on top
- Can be mistaken for golf ball, baseball or even soccer ball

False Parasol
- Poisonous ☹
- White gills with no spores or green gills with green spores
- White to light brown stem

Slippery Jack
- Edible ☺
- Brown cap, shiny and slimy when wet
- Dark chestnut brown
- Smooth semi-matt finish in summer

Spore Print

_____
_____
_____
_____
_____
_____

Location

Site / GPS: _____ Date: _____

○ Living Tree   ○ Leaf Litter   ○ Mulch   ○ Dead Tree or Wood   ○ Grass
○ Soil   ○ Other _____

Type of Tree(s) On or Near: _____

Forest Type: ○ Deciduous   ○ Coniferous   ○ Tropical   ○ Other _____

Weather Conditions: _____

General

Size (overall height): _____   Color: _____   Spore Color: _____

Texture: ○ Tough ○ Brittle ○ Leathery ○ Woody ○ Soft ○ Slimy
○ Spongy ○ Powdery ○ Waxy ○ Rubbery ○ Watery (Other) _____

Bruising When Touched? ○ Yes ○ No   Notes: _____

Structures: ○ Cup ○ Ring ○ Warts   _____

Cap Characteristics

Campanulate
(bell-shaped)

Conical
(triangular)

Cylindrical
(shaped like half an egg)

Convex
(outwardly rounded)

Flat
(with top of
uniform height)

Infundibuliform
(deeply, depressed,
funnel-shaped)

Depressed
(with a low
central region)

Umbonate
(with a central
bump or knob)

Surface Markings (warts, scales, slime, etc.): _____

Cap Margin: Smooth, Inrolled, Sinuous/Wavy, Other:_____

Color Changes: _____

Undercap

Gills ○

Attachment: Free or Decurrent

Spacing: Crowded, Close,
         Distant, Subdistant

Color/Bruising: _____

Pores ○

Color: _____

Pore Size: _____

Pore Pattern: _____

Teeth ○

Color: _____

Teeth Length: _____

Flesh: Soft or Tough

◯ **Free**
(gills not attached to stem)

◯ **Adnexed**
(gills attached narrowly to stem)

◯ **Sinuate**
(gills smoothly notched and running briefly down stem)

◯ **Adnate**
(gills widely attached widely to stem)

◯ **Descending**
(gills running down stem for some length)

    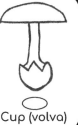

Tapering   **Equal**   **Club-Shaped**   **Bulbous**   **Cup (volva)**

Chanterelle
- Edible ☺
- Shape looks like bell of a trumpet
- Bright yellow/orange
- Similar look to Jack o'Lantern

Meadow Mushroom
- Edible ☺
- White or whitish
- Pink gills that turn brown with age
- Closely related to portobello

Jack O'Lantern
- Poisonous ☹
- Bright orange to yellowish
- Grows in clusters
- Cap convex
- Gills narrow
- Cream spore print

Shaggy Mane
- Edible ☺
- White shaggy cylindrical cap that turns black and inky with age
- Bell shape when mature
- Spore print is black

False Morel
- Poisonous ☹
- Red-brown cap is irregularly lobed, like a brain
- Hollow chambers inside the cap
- Yellowish spore print

Destroying Angel
- Poisonous ☹
- White stalk and gills
- White cap or white edge and yellowish, pinkish, or tan center
- Egg-shaped cap

Morels
- Edible ☺
- Honeycombed cap
- Most morels cap is longer than stem
- Spore print is usually light colored
- Interior is hollow

Fly Agaric
- Poisonous ☹
- Body emerges from soil looking like white eggs and turns red as it grows
- Small white to yellow pyramid-shaped warts

Shaggy Parasol
- Edible ☺
- Thick, fleshy scales on top of cap
- White spores
- White cap
- White gills
- Uniformly colored

Puffballs
- Edible ☺
- Color is white
- Rounded-shaped balls with or without spiny warts on top
- Can be mistaken for golf ball, baseball or even soccer ball

False Parasol
- Poisonous ☹
- White gills with no spores or green gills with green spores
- White to light brown stem

Slippery Jack
- Edible ☺
- Brown cap, shiny and slimy when wet
- Dark chestnut brown
- Smooth semi-matt finish in summer

Spore Print

Location

Site / GPS: _____ Date: _____

○ Living Tree   ○ Leaf Litter   ○ Mulch   ○ Dead Tree or Wood   ○ Grass

○ Soil   ○ Other _____

Type of Tree(s) On or Near: _____

Forest Type: ○ Deciduous   ○ Coniferous   ○ Tropical   ○ Other _____

Weather Conditions: _____

General

Size (overall height): _____   Color: _____   Spore Color: _____

Texture: ○ Tough ○ Brittle ○ Leathery ○ Woody ○ Soft ○ Slimy

○ Spongy   ○ Powdery   ○ Waxy   ○ Rubbery   ○ Watery   (Other) _____

Bruising When Touched? ○ Yes ○ No   Notes: _____

Structures: ○ Cup   ○ Ring   ○ Warts   _____

Cap Characteristics

Campanulate
(bell-shaped)

Conical
(triangular)

Cylindrical
(shaped like half an egg)

Convex
(outwardly rounded)

Flat
(with top of
uniform height)

Infundibuliform
(deeply, depressed,
funnel-shaped)

Depressed
(with a low
central region)

Umbonate
(with a central
bump or knob)

Surface Markings (warts, scales, slime, etc.): _____

Cap Margin: Smooth, Inrolled, Sinuous/Wavy, Other: _____

Color Changes: _____

Undercap

Gills ○

Attachment: Free or Decurrent

Spacing: Crowded, Close,
Distant, Subdistant

Color/Bruising: _____

Pores ○

Color: _____

Pore Size: _____

Pore Pattern: _____

Teeth ○

Color: _____

Teeth Length: _____

Flesh: Soft or Tough

○ **Free**
(gills not attached to stem)

○ **Adnexed**
(gills attached narrowly to stem)

○ **Sinuate**
(gills smoothly notched and running briefly down stem)

○ **Adnate**
(gills widely attached widely to stem)

○ **Descenting**
(gills running down stem for some length)

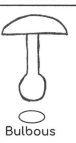

○ **Tapering**

○ **Equal**

○ **Club-Shaped**

○ **Bulbous**

○ **Cup (volva)**

Chanterelle

- Edible ☺
- Shape looks like bell of a trumpet
- Bright yellow/orange
- Similar look to Jack o'Lantern

Meadow Mushroom

- Edible ☺
- White or whitish
- Pink gills that turn brown with age
- Closely related to portobello

Jack O'Lantern

- Poisonous ☹
- Bright orange to yellowish
- Grows in clusters
- Cap convex
- Gills narrow
- Cream spore print

Shaggy Mane

- Edible ☺
- White shaggy cylindrical cap that turns black and inky with age
- Bell shape when mature
- Spore print is black

False Morel

- Poisonous ☹
- Red-brown cap is irregularly lobed, like a brain
- Hollow chambers inside the cap
- Yellowish spore print

Destroying Angel

- Poisonous ☹
- White stalk and gills
- White cap or white edge and yellowish, pinkish, or tan center
- Egg-shaped cap

Morels

- Edible ☺
- Honeycombed cap
- Most morels cap is longer than stem
- Spore print is usually light colored
- Interior is hollow

Fly Agaric

- Poisonous ☹
- Body emerges from soil looking like white eggs and turns red as it grows
- Small white to yellow pyramid-shaped warts

Shaggy Parasol

- Edible ☺
- Thick, fleshy scales on top of cap
- White spores
- White cap
- White gills
- Uniformly colored

Puffballs

- Edible ☺
- Color is white
- Rounded-shaped balls with or without spiny warts on top
- Can be mistaken for golf ball, baseball or even soccer ball

False Parasol

- Poisonous ☹
- White gills with no spores or green gills with green spores
- White to light brown stem

Slippery Jack

- Edible ☺
- Brown cap, shiny and slimy when wet
- Dark chestnut brown
- Smooth semi-matt finish in summer

Spore Print

_____
_____
_____
_____
_____
_____

Location

Site / GPS: _____ Date: _____

◯ Living Tree ◯ Leaf Litter ◯ Mulch ◯ Dead Tree or Wood ◯ Grass
◯ Soil ◯ Other _____

Type of Tree(s) On or Near: _____

Forest Type: ◯ Deciduous ◯ Coniferous ◯ Tropical ◯ Other _____

Weather Conditions: _____

General

Size (overall height): _____ Color: _____ Spore Color: _____

Texture: ◯ Tough ◯ Brittle ◯ Leathery ◯ Woody ◯ Soft ◯ Slimy
◯ Spongy ◯ Powdery ◯ Waxy ◯ Rubbery ◯ Watery (Other) _____

Bruising When Touched? ◯ Yes ◯ No Notes: _____

Structures: ◯ Cup ◯ Ring ◯ Warts _____

Cap Characteristics

Campanulate
(bell-shaped)

Conical
(triangular)

Cylindrical
(shaped like half an egg)

Convex
(outwardly rounded)

Flat
(with top of
uniform height)

Infundibuliform
(deeply, depressed,
funnel-shaped)

Depressed
(with a low
central region)

Umbonate
(with a central
bump or knob)

Surface Markings (warts, scales, slime, etc.): _____

Cap Margin: Smooth, Inrolled, Sinuous/Wavy, Other: _____

Color Changes: _____

Undercap

Gills ◯

Attachment: Free or Decurrent

Spacing: Crowded, Close,
Distant, Subdistant

Color/Bruising: _____

Pores ◯

Color: _____

Pore Size: _____

Pore Pattern: _____

Teeth ◯

Color: _____

Teeth Length: _____

Flesh: Soft or Tough

○ **Free**
(gills not attached to stem)

○ **Adnexed**
(gills attached narrowly to stem)

○ **Sinuate**
(gills smoothly notched and running briefly down stem)

 ○ **Adnate**
(gills widely attached widely to stem)

 ○ **Descenting**
(gills running down stem for some length)

  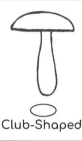  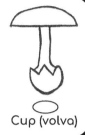

○ **Tapering**   ○ **Equal**   ○ **Club-Shaped**   ○ **Bulbous**   ○ **Cup (volva)**

Chanterelle
- Edible ☺
- Shape looks like bell of a trumpet
- Bright yellow/orange
- Similar look to Jack o'Lantern

Meadow Mushroom
- Edible ☺
- White or whitish
- Pink gills that turn brown with age
- Closely related to portobello

Jack O'Lantern
- Poisonous ☹
- Bright orange to yellowish
- Grows in clusters
- Cap convex
- Gills narrow
- Cream spore print

Shaggy Mane
- Edible ☺
- White shaggy cylindrical cap that turns black and inky with age
- Bell shape when mature
- Spore print is black

False Morel
- Poisonous ☹
- Red-brown cap is irregularly lobed, like a brain
- Hollow chambers inside the cap
- Yellowish spore print

Destroying Angel
- Poisonous ☹
- White stalk and gills
- White cap or white edge and yellowish, pinkish, or tan center
- Egg-shaped cap

Morels
- Edible ☺
- Honeycombed cap
- Most morels cap is longer than stem
- Spore print is usually light colored
- Interior is hollow

Fly Agaric
- Poisonous ☹
- Body emerges from soil looking like white eggs and turns red as it grows
- Small white to yellow pyramid-shaped warts

Shaggy Parasol
- Edible ☺
- Thick, fleshy scales on top of cap
- White spores
- White cap
- White gills
- Uniformly colored

Puffballs
- Edible ☺
- Color is white
- Rounded-shaped balls with or without spiny warts on top
- Can be mistaken for golf ball, baseball or even soccer ball

False Parasol
- Poisonous ☹
- White gills with no spores or green gills with green spores
- White to light brown stem

Slippery Jack
- Edible ☺
- Brown cap, shiny and slimy when wet
- Dark chestnut brown
- Smooth semi-matt finish in summer

Spore Print

_____

_____

_____

_____

_____

_____

Location

Site / GPS: _____ Date: _____

◯ Living Tree ◯ Leaf Litter ◯ Mulch ◯ Dead Tree or Wood ◯ Grass
◯ Soil ◯ Other _____

Type of Tree(s) On or Near: _____

Forest Type: ◯ Deciduous ◯ Coniferous ◯ Tropical ◯ Other _____

Weather Conditions: _____

General

Size (overall height): _____ Color: _____ Spore Color: _____

Texture: ◯ Tough ◯ Brittle ◯ Leathery ◯ Woody ◯ Soft ◯ Slimy
◯ Spongy ◯ Powdery ◯ Waxy ◯ Rubbery ◯ Watery (Other) _____

Bruising When Touched? ◯ Yes ◯ No   Notes: _____

Structures: ◯ Cup ◯ Ring ◯ Warts   _____

Cap Characteristics

Campanulate
(bell-shaped)

Conical
(triangular)

Cylindrical
(shaped like half an egg)

Convex
(outwardly rounded)

Flat
(with top of
uniform height)

Infundibuliform
(deeply, depressed,
funnel-shaped)

Depressed
(with a low
central region)

Umbonate
(with a central
bump or knob)

Surface Markings (warts, scales, slime, etc.): _____

Cap Margin: Smooth, Inrolled, Sinuous/Wavy, Other:_____

Color Changes: _____

Undercap

Gills ◯

Attachment: Free or Decurrent

Spacing: Crowded, Close,
Distant, Subdistant

Color/Bruising: _____

Pores ◯

Color: _____

Pore Size: _____

Pore Pattern: _____

Teeth ◯

Color: _____

Teeth Length: _____

Flesh: Soft or Tough

○ **Free**
(gills not attached to stem)

○ **Adnexed**
(gills attached narrowly to stem)

○ **Sinuate**
(gills smoothly notched and running briefly down stem)

○ **Adnate**
(gills widely attached widely to stem)

○ **Descenting**
(gills running down stem for some length)

○ **Tapering**

○ **Equal**

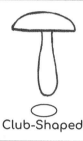

○ **Club-Shaped**

○ **Bulbous**

○ **Cup (volva)**

Chanterelle

- Edible ☺
- Shape looks like bell of a trumpet
- Bright yellow/orange
- Similar look to Jack o'Lantern

Meadow Mushroom

- Edible ☺
- White or whitish
- Pink gills that turn brown with age
- Closely related to portobello

Jack O'Lantern

- Poisonous ☹
- Bright orange to yellowish
- Grows in clusters
- Cap convex
- Gills narrow
- Cream spore print

Shaggy Mane

- Edible ☺
- White shaggy cylindrical cap that turns black and inky with age
- Bell shape when mature
- Spore print is black

False Morel

- Poisonous ☹
- Red-brown cap is irregularly lobed, like a brain
- Hollow chambers inside the cap
- Yellowish spore print

Destroying Angel

- Poisonous ☹
- White stalk and gills
- White cap or white edge and yellowish, pinkish, or tan center
- Egg-shaped cap

Morels

- Edible ☺
- Honeycombed cap
- Most morels cap is longer than stem
- Spore print is usually light colored
- Interior is hollow

Fly Agaric

- Poisonous ☹
- Body emerges from soil looking like white eggs and turns red as it grows
- Small white to yellow pyramid-shaped warts

Shaggy Parasol

- Edible ☺
- Thick, fleshy scales on top of cap
- White spores
- White cap
- White gills
- Uniformly colored

Puffballs

- Edible ☺
- Color is white
- Rounded-shaped balls with or without spiny warts on top
- Can be mistaken for golf ball, baseball or even soccer ball

False Parasol

- Poisonous ☹
- White gills with no spores or green gills with green spores
- White to light brown stem

Slippery Jack

- Edible ☺
- Brown cap, shiny and slimy when wet
- Dark chestnut brown
- Smooth semi-matt finish in summer

Spore Print

Location

Site / GPS: _____ Date: _____

○ Living Tree ○ Leaf Litter ○ Mulch ○ Dead Tree or Wood ○ Grass
○ Soil ○ Other _____

Type of Tree(s) On or Near: _____

Forest Type: ○ Deciduous ○ Coniferous ○ Tropical ○ Other _____

Weather Conditions: _____

General

Size (overall height): _____ Color: _____ Spore Color: _____

Texture: ○ Tough ○ Brittle ○ Leathery ○ Woody ○ Soft ○ Slimy
○ Spongy ○ Powdery ○ Waxy ○ Rubbery ○ Watery (Other) _____

Bruising When Touched? ○ Yes ○ No   Notes: _____

Structures: ○ Cup ○ Ring ○ Warts   _____

Cap Characteristics

Campanulate
(bell-shaped)

Conical
(triangular)

Cylindrical
(shaped like half an egg)

Convex
(outwardly rounded)

Flat
(with top of
uniform height)

Infundibuliform
(deeply, depressed,
funnel-shaped)

Depressed
(with a low
central region)

Umbonate
(with a central
bump or knob)

Surface Markings (warts, scales, slime, etc.): _____

Cap Margin: Smooth, Inrolled, Sinuous/Wavy, Other:_____

Color Changes: _____

Undercap

Gills ○
Attachment: Free or Decurrent
Spacing: Crowded, Close,
Distant, Subdistant
Color/Bruising: _____

Pores ○
Color: _____
Pore Size: _____
Pore Pattern: _____

Teeth ○
Color: _____
Teeth Length: _____
Flesh: Soft or Tough

○ Free
(gills not attached to stem)

○ Adnexed
(gills attached narrowly to stem)

○ Sinuate
(gills smoothly notched and running briefly down stem)

○ Adnate
(gills widely attached widely to stem)

○ Descenting
(gills running down stem for some length)

  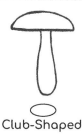 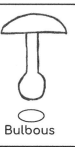 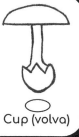

○ Tapering

○ Equal

○ Club-Shaped

○ Bulbous

○ Cup (volva)

Chanterelle
- Edible ☺
- Shape looks like bell of a trumpet
- Bright yellow/orange
- Similar look to Jack o'Lantern

Meadow Mushroom
- Edible ☺
- White or whitish
- Pink gills that turn brown with age
- Closely related to portobello

Jack O'Lantern
- Poisonous ☹
- Bright orange to yellowish
- Grows in clusters
- Cap convex
- Gills narrow
- Cream spore print

Shaggy Mane
- Edible ☺
- White shaggy cylindrical cap that turns black and inky with age
- Bell shape when mature
- Spore print is black

False Morel
- Poisonous ☹
- Red-brown cap is irregularly lobed, like a brain
- Hollow chambers inside the cap
- Yellowish spore print

Destroying Angel
- Poisonous ☹
- White stalk and gills
- White cap or white edge and yellowish, pinkish, or tan center
- Egg-shaped cap

Morels
- Edible ☺
- Honeycombed cap
- Most morels cap is longer than stem
- Spore print is usually light colored
- Interior is hollow

Fly Agaric
- Poisonous ☹
- Body emerges from soil looking like white eggs and turns red as it grows
- Small white to yellow pyramid-shaped warts

Shaggy Parasol
- Edible ☺
- Thick, fleshy scales on top of cap
- White spores
- White cap
- White gills
- Uniformly colored

Puffballs
- Edible ☺
- Color is white
- Rounded-shaped balls with or without spiny warts on top
- Can be mistaken for golf ball, baseball or even soccer ball

False Parasol
- Poisonous ☹
- White gills with no spores or green gills with green spores
- White to light brown stem

Slippery Jack
- Edible ☺
- Brown cap, shiny and slimy when wet
- Dark chestnut brown
- Smooth semi-matt finish in summer

Spore Print

_____
_____
_____
_____
_____
_____

Location

Site / GPS: _____   Date: _____

○ Living Tree   ○ Leaf Litter   ○ Mulch   ○ Dead Tree or Wood   ○ Grass
○ Soil   ○ Other _____

Type of Tree(s) On or Near: _____

Forest Type: ○ Deciduous   ○ Coniferous   ○ Tropical   ○ Other _____

Weather Conditions: _____

General

Size (overall height): _____   Color: _____   Spore Color: _____

Texture: ○ Tough ○ Brittle ○ Leathery ○ Woody ○ Soft ○ Slimy
○ Spongy   ○ Powdery   ○ Waxy   ○ Rubbery   ○ Watery   (Other) _____

Bruising When Touched? ○ Yes ○ No   Notes: _____

Structures: ○ Cup   ○ Ring   ○ Warts   _____

Cap Characteristics

Campanulate
(bell-shaped)

Conical
(triangular)

Cylindrical
(shaped like half an egg)

Convex
(outwardly rounded)

Flat
(with top of
uniform height)

Infundibuliform
(deeply, depressed,
funnel-shaped)

Depressed
(with a low
central region)

Umbonate
(with a central
bump or knob)

Surface Markings (warts, scales, slime, etc.): _____

Cap Margin: Smooth, Inrolled, Sinuous/Wavy, Other: _____

Color Changes: _____

Undercap

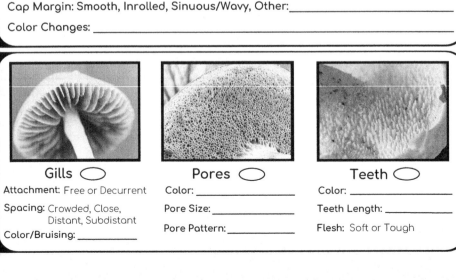

Gills ○

Attachment: Free or Decurrent

Spacing: Crowded, Close,
           Distant, Subdistant

Color/Bruising: _____

Pores ○

Color: _____

Pore Size: _____

Pore Pattern: _____

Teeth ○

Color: _____

Teeth Length: _____

Flesh: Soft or Tough

◯ **Free**
(gills not attached to stem)

◯ **Adnexed**
(gills attached narrowly to stem)

◯ **Sinuate**
(gills smoothly notched and running briefly down stem)

◯ **Adnate**
(gills widely attached widely to stem)

◯ **Descenting**
(gills running down stem for some length)

 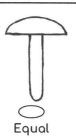   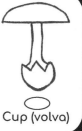

◯ **Tapering**   ◯ **Equal**   ◯ **Club-Shaped**   ◯ **Bulbous**   ◯ **Cup (volva)**

Chanterelle
- Edible ☺
- Shape looks like bell of a trumpet
- Bright yellow/orange
- Similar look to Jack o'Lantern

Meadow Mushroom
- Edible ☺
- White or whitish
- Pink gills that turn brown with age
- Closely related to portobello

Jack O'Lantern
- Poisonous ☹
- Bright orange to yellowish
- Grows in clusters
- Cap convex
- Gills narrow
- Cream spore print

Shaggy Mane
- Edible ☺
- White shaggy cylindrical cap that turns black and inky with age
- Bell shape when mature
- Spore print is black

False Morel
- Poisonous ☹
- Red-brown cap is irregularly lobed, like a brain
- Hollow chambers inside the cap
- Yellowish spore print

Destroying Angel
- Poisonous ☹
- White stalk and gills
- White cap or white edge and yellowish, pinkish, or tan center
- Egg-shaped cap

Morels
- Edible ☺
- Honeycombed cap
- Most morels cap is longer than stem
- Spore print is usually light colored
- Interior is hollow

Fly Agaric
- Poisonous ☹
- Body emerges from soil looking like white eggs and turns red as it grows
- Small white to yellow pyramid-shaped warts

Shaggy Parasol
- Edible ☺
- Thick, fleshy scales on top of cap
- White spores
- White cap
- White gills
- Uniformly colored

Puffballs
- Edible ☺
- Color is white
- Rounded-shaped balls with or without spiny warts on top
- Can be mistaken for golf ball, baseball or even soccer ball

False Parasol
- Poisonous ☹
- White gills with no spores or green gills with green spores
- White to light brown stem

Slippery Jack
- Edible ☺
- Brown cap, shiny and slimy when wet
- Dark chestnut brown
- Smooth semi-matt finish in summer

Spore Print

_____
_____
_____
_____
_____
_____

Location

Site / GPS: _____ Date: _____

○ Living Tree   ○ Leaf Litter   ○ Mulch   ○ Dead Tree or Wood   ○ Grass
○ Soil   ○ Other _____

Type of Tree(s) On or Near: _____

Forest Type: ○ Deciduous   ○ Coniferous   ○ Tropical   ○ Other _____

Weather Conditions: _____

General

Size (overall height): _____   Color: _____   Spore Color: _____

Texture: ○ Tough   ○ Brittle   ○ Leathery   ○ Woody   ○ Soft   ○ Slimy
○ Spongy   ○ Powdery   ○ Waxy   ○ Rubbery   ○ Watery   (Other)_____

Bruising When Touched? ○ Yes   ○ No   Notes: _____

Structures: ○ Cup   ○ Ring   ○ Warts   _____

Cap Characteristics

Campanulate
(bell-shaped)

Conical
(triangular)

Cylindrical
(shaped like half an egg)

Convex
(outwardly rounded)

Flat
(with top of
uniform height)

Infundibuliform
(deeply, depressed,
funnel-shaped)

Depressed
(with a low
central region)

Umbonate
(with a central
bump or knob)

Surface Markings (warts, scales, slime, etc.): _____

Cap Margin: Smooth, Inrolled, Sinuous/Wavy, Other:_____

Color Changes: _____

Undercap

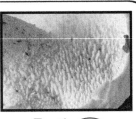

Gills ○

Attachment: Free or Decurrent

Spacing: Crowded, Close,
Distant, Subdistant

Color/Bruising: _____

Pores ○

Color: _____

Pore Size: _____

Pore Pattern: _____

Teeth ○

Color: _____

Teeth Length: _____

Flesh: Soft or Tough

 Free
(gills not attached to stem)

 Adnexed
(gills attached narrowly to stem)

Sinuate
(gills smoothly notched and running briefly down stem)

Adnate
(gills widely attached widely to stem)

 Descenting
(gills running down stem for some length)

 Tapering

 Equal

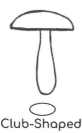 Club-Shaped

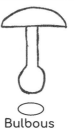 Bulbous

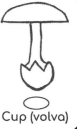 Cup (volva)

Chanterelle

- Edible ☺
- Shape looks like bell of a trumpet
- Bright yellow/orange
- Similar look to Jack o'Lantern

Meadow Mushroom

- Edible ☺
- White or whitish
- Pink gills that turn brown with age
- Closely related to portobello

Jack O'Lantern

- Poisonous ☹
- Bright orange to yellowish
- Grows in clusters
- Cap convex
- Gills narrow
- Cream spore print

Shaggy Mane

- Edible ☺
- White shaggy cylindrical cap that turns black and inky with age
- Bell shape when mature
- Spore print is black

False Morel

- Poisonous ☹
- Red-brown cap is irregularly lobed, like a brain
- Hollow chambers inside the cap
- Yellowish spore print

Destroying Angel

- Poisonous ☹
- White stalk and gills
- White cap or white edge and yellowish, pinkish, or tan center
- Egg-shaped cap

Morels

- Edible ☺
- Honeycombed cap
- Most morels cap is longer than stem
- Spore print is usually light colored
- Interior is hollow

Fly Agaric

- Poisonous ☹
- Body emerges from soil looking like white eggs and turns red as it grows
- Small white to yellow pyramid-shaped warts

Shaggy Parasol

- Edible ☺
- Thick, fleshy scales on top of cap
- White spores
- White cap
- White gills
- Uniformly colored

Puffballs

- Edible ☺
- Color is white
- Rounded-shaped balls with or without spiny warts on top
- Can be mistaken for golf ball, baseball or even soccer ball

False Parasol

- Poisonous ☹
- White gills with no spores or green gills with green spores
- White to light brown stem

Slippery Jack

- Edible ☺
- Brown cap, shiny and slimy when wet
- Dark chestnut brown
- Smooth semi-matt finish in summer

Spore Print

Location

Site / GPS: _____ Date: _____

○ Living Tree   ○ Leaf Litter   ○ Mulch   ○ Dead Tree or Wood   ○ Grass
○ Soil   ○ Other _____

Type of Tree(s) On or Near: _____

Forest Type: ○ Deciduous   ○ Coniferous   ○ Tropical   ○ Other _____

Weather Conditions: _____

General

Size (overall height): _____   Color: _____   Spore Color: _____

Texture: ○ Tough ○ Brittle ○ Leathery ○ Woody ○ Soft ○ Slimy
○ Spongy ○ Powdery ○ Waxy ○ Rubbery ○ Watery (Other) _____

Bruising When Touched? ○ Yes ○ No   Notes: _____

Structures: ○ Cup ○ Ring ○ Warts   _____

Cap Characteristics

Campanulate
(bell-shaped)

Conical
(triangular)

Cylindrical
(shaped like half an egg)

Convex
(outwardly rounded)

Flat
(with top of
uniform height)

Infundibuliform
(deeply, depressed,
funnel-shaped)

Depressed
(with a low
central region)

Umbonate
(with a central
bump or knob)

Surface Markings (warts, scales, slime, etc.): _____

Cap Margin: Smooth, Inrolled, Sinuous/Wavy, Other:_____

Color Changes: _____

Undercap

Gills ○

Attachment: Free or Decurrent

Spacing: Crowded, Close,
        Distant, Subdistant

Color/Bruising: _____

Pores ○

Color: _____

Pore Size: _____

Pore Pattern: _____

Teeth ○

Color: _____

Teeth Length: _____

Flesh: Soft or Tough

Gill Attachment

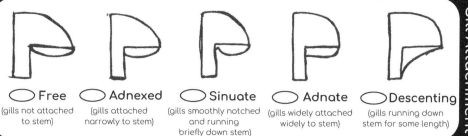

- **Free** (gills not attached to stem)
- **Adnexed** (gills attached narrowly to stem)
- **Sinuate** (gills smoothly notched and running briefly down stem)
- **Adnate** (gills widely attached widely to stem)
- **Descenting** (gills running down stem for some length)

Stem Shape

  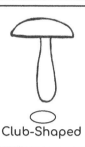 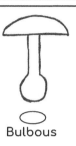 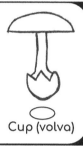

- **Tapering**
- **Equal**
- **Club-Shaped**
- **Bulbous**
- **Cup (volva)**

Common Mushrooms

Chanterelle
- Edible ☺
- Shape looks like bell of a trumpet
- Bright yellow/orange
- Similar look to Jack o'Lantern

Meadow Mushroom
- Edible ☺
- White or whitish
- Pink gills that turn brown with age
- Closely related to portobello

Jack O'Lantern
- Poisonous ☹
- Bright orange to yellowish
- Grows in clusters
- Cap convex
- Gills narrow
- Cream spore print

Shaggy Mane
- Edible ☺
- White shaggy cylindrical cap that turns black and inky with age
- Bell shape when mature
- Spore print is black

False Morel
- Poisonous ☹
- Red-brown cap is irregularly lobed, like a brain
- Hollow chambers inside the cap
- Yellowish spore print

Destroying Angel
- Poisonous ☹
- White stalk and gills
- White cap or white edge and yellowish, pinkish, or tan center
- Egg-shaped cap

Morels
- Edible ☺
- Honeycombed cap
- Most morels cap is longer than stem
- Spore print is usually light colored
- Interior is hollow

Fly Agaric
- Poisonous ☹
- Body emerges from soil looking like white eggs and turns red as it grows
- Small white to yellow pyramid-shaped warts

Shaggy Parasol
- Edible ☺
- Thick, fleshy scales on top of cap
- White spores
- White cap
- White gills
- Uniformly colored

Puffballs
- Edible ☺
- Color is white
- Rounded-shaped balls with or without spiny warts on top
- Can be mistaken for golf ball, baseball or even soccer ball

False Parasol
- Poisonous ☹
- White gills with no spores or green gills with green spores
- White to light brown stem

Slippery Jack
- Edible ☺
- Brown cap, shiny and slimy when wet
- Dark chestnut brown
- Smooth semi-matt finish in summer

Spore Print

Notes

_____
_____
_____
_____
_____
_____

Location

Site / GPS: _____ Date: _____

○ Living Tree ○ Leaf Litter ○ Mulch ○ Dead Tree or Wood ○ Grass
○ Soil ○ Other _____

Type of Tree(s) On or Near: _____

Forest Type: ○ Deciduous ○ Coniferous ○ Tropical ○ Other _____

Weather Conditions: _____

General

Size (overall height): _____ Color: _____ Spore Color: _____

Texture: ○ Tough ○ Brittle ○ Leathery ○ Woody ○ Soft ○ Slimy
○ Spongy ○ Powdery ○ Waxy ○ Rubbery ○ Watery (Other) _____

Bruising When Touched? ○ Yes ○ No Notes: _____

Structures: ○ Cup ○ Ring ○ Warts _____

Cap Characteristics

Campanulate
(bell-shaped)

Conical
(triangular)

Cylindrical
(shaped like half an egg)

Convex
(outwardly rounded)

Flat
(with top of
uniform height)

Infundibuliform
(deeply, depressed,
funnel-shaped)

Depressed
(with a low
central region)

Umbonate
(with a central
bump or knob)

Surface Markings (warts, scales, slime, etc.): _____

Cap Margin: Smooth, Inrolled, Sinuous/Wavy, Other: _____

Color Changes: _____

Undercap

Gills ○

Attachment: Free or Decurrent

Spacing: Crowded, Close,
Distant, Subdistant

Color/Bruising: _____

Pores ○

Color: _____

Pore Size: _____

Pore Pattern: _____

Teeth ○

Color: _____

Teeth Length: _____

Flesh: Soft or Tough

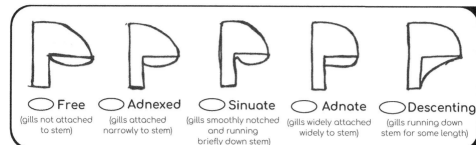

○ Free
(gills not attached to stem)

○ Adnexed
(gills attached narrowly to stem)

○ Sinuate
(gills smoothly notched and running briefly down stem)

○ Adnate
(gills widely attached widely to stem)

○ Descenting
(gills running down stem for some length)

  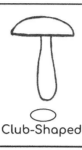  

Tapering — Equal — Club-Shaped — Bulbous — Cup (volva)

Chanterelle
- Edible ☺
- Shape looks like bell of a trumpet
- Bright yellow/orange
- Similar look to Jack o'Lantern

Shaggy Mane
- Edible ☺
- White shaggy cylindrical cap that turns black and inky with age
- Bell shape when mature
- Spore print is black

Morels
- Edible ☺
- Honeycombed cap
- Most morels cap is longer than stem
- Spore print is usually light colored
- Interior is hollow

Puffballs
- Edible ☺
- Color is white
- Rounded-shaped balls with or without spiny warts on top
- Can be mistaken for golf ball, baseball or even soccer ball

Meadow Mushroom
- Edible ☺
- White or whitish
- Pink gills that turn brown with age
- Closely related to portobello

False Morel
- Poisonous ☹
- Red-brown cap is irregularly lobed, like a brain
- Hollow chambers inside the cap
- Yellowish spore print

Fly Agaric
- Poisonous ☹
- Body emerges from soil looking like white eggs and turns red as it grows
- Small white to yellow pyramid-shaped warts

False Parasol
- Poisonous ☹
- White gills with no spores or green gills with green spores
- White to light brown stem

Jack O'Lantern
- Poisonous ☹
- Bright orange to yellowish
- Grows in clusters
- Cap convex
- Gills narrow
- Cream spore print

Destroying Angel
- Poisonous ☹
- White stalk and gills
- White cap or white edge and yellowish, pinkish, or tan center
- Egg-shaped cap

Shaggy Parasol
- Edible ☺
- Thick, fleshy scales on top of cap
- White spores
- White cap
- White gills
- Uniformly colored

Slippery Jack
- Edible ☺
- Brown cap, shiny and slimy when wet
- Dark chestnut brown
- Smooth semi-matt finish in summer

Spore Print

_____
_____
_____
_____
_____
_____

Made in the USA
Middletown, DE
12 June 2022

67020635R00066